*The Poems of Alcimus Ecdicius Avitus*

———————————————

# MEDIEVAL & RENAISSANCE

# TEXTS & STUDIES

## VOLUME 172

# The Poems of Alcimus Ecdicius Avitus

Translation and Introduction

BY

GEORGE W. SHEA

MEDIEVAL & RENAISSANCE TEXTS & STUDIES
Tempe, Arizona
1997

**Library of Congress Cataloging-in-Publication Data**

Avitus, Saint, Bishop of Vienne.
    The poems of Alcimus Ecdicius Avitus / translation and introduction by
George W. Shea.
       p.   cm. — (Medieval & Renaissance text & studies ; v. 172)
    Includes bibliographical references (p.  ) and index.
    ISBN 0-86698-214-0
    1. Christian poetry, Latin (Medieval and modern) — Translations into
English. 2. Bible. O.T. — History of Biblical events — Poetry. 3. Virginity —
Religious aspects — Poetry. 4. Fall of man — Poetry.
I. Shea, George W. II. Title. III. Series.
PA6229.A9A27 1997
873'.01—dc21                                          96–52898
                                                        CIP

∞

This book was edited and produced
by MRTS at SUNY Binghamton.
This book has been made to last.
It is set in Garamond Antiqua typeface,
smyth-sewn, and printed on acid-free paper
to library specifications.

Printed in the United States of America

# Table of Contents

*For Shirley*

# *Preface*

The poems of Alcimus Ecdicius Avitus are of interest not only to students of late Latin and early Christian literature but to those studying history, philosophy and theology as well. For comparatists the text is especially interesting, particularly for those examining epic poetry and the reworking of classical epic structures and techniques by later authors. Unfortunately, for many students in these fields the Latin text is not accessible. For this reason, I decided to translate the poems into English. Since I assumed that my readers would be largely Latinless students and scholars, I have attempted to keep my translation as close to the original text as possible, struggling at the same time to hold to a natural and readable English prose style. I have not attempted to improve Avitus, who is only rarely, it must be admitted, a poet of the first rank. Occasionally, I have provided a missing proper name, demonstrative or explanatory phrase to help the reader through an ambiguous passage. I have not attempted to reproduce the author's extensive use of the historical present tense, which is somewhat awkward when translated into English, particularly when there are frequent shifts from one tense to another. Finally, I have taken some liberties with Avitus' highly complex and hypotactic style, realigning syntactical subordinations in the interest of clarity and readability, without, I trust, altering the meaning of the text.

My introduction is not meant to function as a formal commentary on Avitus' text; such a work still remains to be done. Rather, I try in it to give the reader an overview of the narrative and of the structure of the poems, providing at the same time some idea of the poet's sensibility, technique and diction. For this reason, I discuss the collection poem by poem, quoting frequently from the Latin text. I have also considered what I see as major themes in Avitus' poems and have attempted to trace the thread of their development through the entire corpus.

The reader should be aware of two limitations which the length, scope and purpose of the introduction have imposed. First, I do not attempt an analysis of Avitus' treatment of the theological controversies of his age, in spite of the fact that there are echoes of these in the poems. Such a study would require consideration of his letters and sermons, as well as a thorough knowledge of a broad range of theological texts by earlier and contemporary authors. Second, and perhaps more important, I have not attempted a systematic comparison of Avitus' narrative either with his scriptural sources or with other authors who dealt with biblical narrative. I have normally indicated the sources in scripture for both the narrative and for the large digressions and have, when differences in treatment seemed particularly interesting or illustrative of a major thematic concern, pointed these out. The same holds true for references to other biblical poets in my notes, which should not be considered an exhaustive treatment of Avitus' relationship to these authors. For further treatment of biblical paraphrase and poetry, the reader may wish to consult the works of Herzog, Kartschoke and Roberts listed in the bibliography.

My translation is based upon the text of Peiper in Mon. Germ. Hist., Auct. Antiqu. 6.2. I found it necessary to dispute his readings very rarely. The following is a list of the emendations of his text which I have adopted:

Prol. 2.12: *tutius* for *totius* (Peiper corrigenda)
1.76: *cuius* for *quibus*
1.292: *flamina* for *flumina*
2.48: *primas* for *primus* (Peiper corrigenda)
3.17: *aluit* for *rapit*
3.123: *trepida* for *trepido*
4.12: *cuique* for *quisque*
4.472: *salsis* for *Falsis*
4.587: *seris* for *serris*
5.83: *quos talia* for *hostilia*
5.343: *secum dimissa ferat* for *tecum dimisse feras*
5.633: *abeant* for *habeant*
6.101: *superanti* for *superantes*
6.537: *convictus* for *confictus*
6.590: *totos* for *totus*
6.634: *petetur* for *petatur*
6.664: *cum* for *dum*

Changes in punctuation are not included in this list.

References to late Greek and Latin authors in the notes are to Migne, *Patrologia Graeca* or *Patrologia Latina*, henceforth *P.G.* or *P.L.*

Line numbers at the top of the pages of the Translation and in the Index of Proper Names refer to the Latin text.

I would like to thank my wife, Shirley Ashton Shea, for her invaluable help in proofreading this text and my colleagues at Fordham University for their assistance and advice. Finally, I would like to thank the anonymous readers at Medieval & Renaissance Texts & Studies for their many corrections and helpful advice.

# Introduction

## Life and Works

The precise birthdate of Alcimus Ecdicius Avitus is unknown, but we may safely assume that he was born sometime in the middle of the fifth century, probably not long after AD 450. His family belonged to the Gallo-Roman aristocracy. They held senatorial status and were, it seems likely, related to the Emperor Avitus (455–456) and to his son-in-law, the poet, Sidonius Apollinaris. Avitus' own father, Isicius, was himself the bishop of Vienne, the post to which our poet was elected in AD 494. His mother's name was Audentia. His brother, the namesake of the poet Sidonius Apollinaris, was named the bishop of Valence and was, Avitus tells us, instrumental in securing the publication of his poetry, including the sixth poem, which is addressed to his sister, Fuscina, who was a nun.[1]

An energetic leader of the Church in Gaul, Avitus presided over the Council of Epao in AD 517 and led the struggle against Arianism, to which the Burgundian King, Gundobad, had given his allegiance. He

---

[1] For the life of Avitus see, in addition to his own works: Ennodius, *Vita B. Epiphanii* (*P.L.* 63:234); Gregory of Tours, *Historia Francorum* 2:34 (*P.L.* 71:230); Isidore of Seville, *de Viris Illustribus* 36 (*P.L.* 83:1101); Agobard of Lyons, *Adversum Legem Gundobadi* (*P.L.* 104:124); Ado of Vienne, *Chronicon Aetatis Sextae* (*P.L.* 123:105). The precise relationship of our poet to the emperor Avitus cannot be determined. However, since Avitus writes to the emperor's grandson, employing terms like *parentum communium sortem* and *nostra familia*, it is likely that the emperor was either his grandfather or great-uncle. To the next generation belong Avitus' father, Isicius, who succeeded the poet's godfather, Mamertus, as bishop of Vienne, and the emperor's son, Ecdicius, and son-in-law, the poet Sidonius Apollinaris, who was also the bishop of Clermont. The third generation, to which our poet belongs, includes two figures by the name of Sidonius Apollinaris: Avitus' brother, the bishop of Valence and the son of the above-mentioned poet, to whom one of Avitus' letters is addressed.

was responsible for the conversion to orthodoxy of the heir to the Burgundian throne, Sigismund. He died not long after the Council of Epao, probably in AD 518.

His literary corpus includes the six poems[2] that are the subject of this volume, five of which are renderings in verse of biblical narrative and bear the title *De spiritualis historiae gestis*. The sixth, which is addressed to his sister, was written in praise of chastity and the celibate state. In addition, a collection of letters and some of his sermons survive. The letters, which fall into the period stretching from AD 495 to AD 517, deal with theological and moral questions. Many are addressed to prominent political figures: to Kings Gundobad and Clovis, to Gundobad's heir, Sigismund, and to the Roman senators, Faustus and Symmachus. Of the thirty-four known sermons, fragments of thirty-one survive. Only three have been preserved in their entirety, two dealing with the observation of the Rogation Days in Vienne,[3] one celebrating the consecration of the Church of St. Maurice in Agaunum.[4]

## The Structure of the Collection

To Avitus' collection of six poems two prologues addressed to his brother, Sidonius Apollinaris, are added. The first introduces the first five poems, the second, the sixth and final poem. The reason for this arrangement is obvious: the first five poems present a related series of biblical narratives; the sixth, which was written at a later date, was composed for a specific occasion and is a meditative rather than a narrative work. The biblical poems are ordered chronologically. The first three present an account of the Creation, the Fall and the Judgement of Adam and Eve, as well as an account of their banishment from Eden. The fourth poem contains the story of the Flood and the preservation of Noah and his family. The fifth is Avitus' version of the Exodus of the

---

[2] Should the five books of the *De spiritualis historiae gestis* (*S.H.G.*) be referred to as poems? They clearly form a single work. On the other hand, Avitus refers to them in his prologue in the plural. I have decided to use the term "poem" of each while recognizing at the same time that they are part of a larger whole.

[3] This ceremonial was instituted by Avitus' godfather Mamertus, while he was bishop of Vienne. Gregory, *Historia Francorum* 2:34 (*P.L.* 71:231)

[4] This church was built by the Burgundian prince, Sigismund, the son of King Gundobad. Gregory, *Historia Francorum* 3:5 (*P.L.* 71:244).

Hebrew people from Egypt and includes an account of the parting of the Red Sea and the destruction of the Egyptian army.

The sixth poem, Avitus' poetic study of and exhortation to the practice of chastity, is, as we noted above, addressed to his sister, Fuscina. This poem presents many examples of chaste women, including several within Avitus' own family, and contrasts the married and religious states. The sixth poem also explores chastity's foundation in both faith and good deeds and its relationship to the Christian economy of grace.

An initial reading of Avitus' six poems suggests little unifying purpose or structure. The first three biblical poems present, it is true, a coherent story of the Creation, Fall and Judgement, albeit with a number of digressions. The subjects of the fourth and fifth poems involve an apparent leap in the historical sequence, and the final poem seems completely unrelated to those which precede it. Closer examination, however, reveals three underlying themes or concerns in Avitus' poetry, concerns that give the reader additional perspectives from which to view the relation of the poems to one another.

First, the poems are a presentation of the Christian view of human history and the conditions of mankind in the various periods of that history. Seen from this point of view, the poems present a vision of the human race at certain crucial points in the unfolding of the divine plan for salvation. The first three poems contain an account of the creation of mankind and of the condition of pre-and post-lapsarian humanity. The fourth book presents mankind at its lowest point of spiritual degeneration, that reached just prior to the flood. In the account of the Exodus of the Jews, a new and more positive stage of human history is described, that which presents the salvation and formation of the people from whom the Redeemer would come. The sixth poem, although not linked by the author himself to the first five, in fact presents the condition of mankind after its redemption. Avitus, Fuscina and their family are the types of the new Christian, members of the Church militant, awaiting the Second Coming of Christ. The central event in this historical framework, the Redemption itself, is not treated by Avitus in a separate poem. It is not, however, entirely absent from his presentation of human history. As we might expect, the Redemption is prominent in all of the poems, either foreshadowed or recalled. It is presented as the preeminently significant event, that which provides the key for the interpretation of all the other acts which the poet narrates.

The second theme that permeates all of the poems is hermeneutic and literary. Avitus was not only a Christian bishop whose family members had for generations been numbered among the princes of the Church; he was also a member of the Gallo-Roman aristocracy and had received the education to which that membership entitled him. He was, his works indicate, familiar with Latin literary classics, with Greek and Roman myth, and with the ideas of Greek philosophy. Thus, like many Christian intellectuals before him, he was faced with the question of the relationship of the Christian to the Graeco-Roman vision, of the Gospel to ancient myth and, as a writer, of the Christian use of metaphor and parable to the rhetoric of the Greeks and Romans.[5]

Quite naturally, then, one of the central themes in Avitus' poems is the nature and status of human knowledge and discourse. He was aware of the pagan charges of Christian literary and philosophical naïveté and therefore took pains to demonstrate his familiarity with the classics of Greece and Rome. It is clear, however, that he viewed the ancient pagan philosophical and literary enterprise as a hermeneutical system irreconcilable with the Christian point of view. The vision of human history outlined above occupied for him a privileged position. It provided for the believer the key to understanding all phenomena. That key was, quite simply, the Redemption and the *eschaton* to which it pointed, that final moment in human history at which the divine plan is brought to fulfillment. In view of this, both the rational speculation of ancient philosophy and, more importantly for the poet Avitus, the mythic discourse of ancient literature, could not but be judged as inferior hermeneutical techniques whose analysis of the significance of phenomenal and noumenal worlds was largely false. Furthermore, Avitus, unlike other Christian poets of the period,[6] rejected much of the apparatus and imagery of his classical models. As a result, he rarely employed the mythological framework of earlier Latin poets, and when these mythic

---

[5] For the attitudes of earlier and contemporary Christian thinkers to Greek myth, see Methodius, *The Symposium* 8:14 (*P.G.* 18:161–65), and Augustine, *Civitas Dei* 18:12 (*P.L.* 41:569ff).

[6] Christian poets of this period vary widely in their use of Greek myth. Sidonius Apollinaris employs it throughout his poems and rejects the Greek Muses only when addressing a bishop, *Carmina* 16:1–5 (*P.L.* 58:718). Dracontius, like Avitus, refers to myth as *fabula mendax*, used in the service of a *numen vanum* with whom he contrasts the true God *de quo nil fingitur*, *Carmen de Deo* 3:513–20 (*P.L.* 60:885–86). Earlier, Sedulius likewise contrasted the content of pagan and Christian verse, using *mendacia* of the former, *Carmen Paschale* 1:17–59 (*P.L.* 19:553–59). For the practice of the sixth-century African poet, Flavius Cresconius Corippus, see my "Myth and Religion in an Early Christian Epic," *Medieval Studies*, 35 (1973): 118–35.

structures were referred to, Avitus took care to brand them as false and unworthy of belief.

Avitus concerned himself as well with the crude pseudo-science and superstition of his day and its attempts to explain and control the phenomenal world through various kinds of observation, the application of traditional wisdom and, not infrequently, the practice of magic. This pseudo-science was in fact a mixture of facts, theories, legends and practices drawn from a broad range of sources. Although it reveals some traces of Greek and Roman science, the larger portion of it is drawn from literary works or from the realm of folk wisdom and magic. Avitus' reaction to this approach to the natural world is ambivalent, for although he condemns again and again human *curiositas* and mankind's attempts, whether technological or magical, to meddle in the divine disposition of the world, he also manifests in many places the very *curiositas* which he condemns. It is not always easy to distinguish between the merely decorative use of such material and a genuinely empirical, albeit naïve scientific impulse. As we review the individual poems, however, we shall find evidence of a mind to some degree at odds with itself in this regard. The bishop condemns *curiositas* as he must, but the poet, with his lively imagination, enjoys speculation about the natural world and delights in setting it forth in his work.[7]

---

[7] On the Church's hostility and indifference to science as well as the influence of superstition and the mystery cults, see Benjamin Farrington, *Science in Antiquity* (Oxford: Oxford Univ. Press, 1969), 135-36. For a more extensive treatment of the sensibilities of fifth-century Christian intellectuals and their attitudes toward speculation about the natural world, see H. Marrou, *Saint Augustin et la fin de la culture antique* (Paris, 1938). Marrou uses Augustine to demonstrate that the "science" of this age was drawn largely from books (15, 137) and included little more than an inorganic mass of facts (120), the knowledge of which might give immediate pleasure (150) but did not aim at the production of scientific laws (137) or at what we would call scientific progress (152). Quite the contrary, he suggests that interest in the natural world often focused on the bizarre, extraordinary and inexplicable (155-57). He concludes that for Augustine and his contemporary Christians science in the modern sense was not practiced (107), that, in fact, "la *scientia* ce n'est pas seulement un usage inferieur, mais un usage pervers et coupable de raison; c'est le mouvement de l'âme qui se detourne de la consideration de Dieu et s'attache a la connaissance des réalités terrestres" ("Science is not only an inferior practice but a practice that is perverse and rationally blameworthy; it is a movement of the soul, which turns away from the consideration of God and directs itself to the understanding of earthly realities"—371). He provides several illustrative quotes from Augustine himself, among them: "illa namque quae de hoc mundo quaeruntur nec satis ad beatam vitam obtinendam mihi videtur pertinere." ("For those truths which are sought for in earthly investigation are not, it seems to me, relevant to securing a blessed life."—*Letter to Nebridius* 11:2 [*P.L.* 33:75]) and of scientific speculation: "ne obscura et non necessaria quaestio nos fatiget" ("so that a search both unclear and unnecessary not weary us."—*Civitas Dei* 15:2 [*P.L.* 41:457]). I would argue that, although Avitus shares this sensibility to some degree, his poems demonstrate some genuine interest

The third theme that runs through all six of the poems may be found in the poet's treatment of the relationship of matter to spirit, of the physical world to the world of mind, will and grace. Throughout his biblical narrative and on into the sixth poem, Avitus displays a curiosity not only about matter and the physical world, but most especially, about its relationship to evil. With the creation of Eve, for example, we find the suggestion that matter is particularly susceptible to the influence of the satanic (1.160), and in the poems that follow the Fall, Avitus focuses again and again on the degeneration of the physical world, on the moral implications of that degeneration, and also on physical processes themselves. And nowhere is this interest in physical processes and their moral implications more prominent than in his treatment of human procreation and sexuality. In his description of Satan's temptation of Eve and of God's judgement, he introduces the idea of the susceptibility of woman to seduction (2.145–66), and then dwells upon the darkness of post-lapsarian sexuality (3.137–52). In the final poem, these topics are among his central preoccupations. There, in his study of the condition of mankind after its redemption, Avitus presents both a theological and sociological-psychological study of sexuality in his age. His text carries, on the surface at least, a severe but largely orthodox view of sexuality, marriage and procreation. These biological processes and states of life are presented as clearly inferior to the practice of celibacy and the asceticism meant to accompany it. What is more, sexuality is presented as an obstacle to the attainment of sanctity.[8] Behind this orthodox view of the place of sexuality in human history and in the individual's quest

---

in speculation about the natural world. I base this hypothesis on three facts: the frequency of such interest in his text, the apparent foundation of some of his speculation on observation rather than literary sources and the frequent insistence on the orthodox view presented above, which belies, I believe, an uneasy conscience. If my hypothesis is correct, one might further ask whence this interest in the natural world came. It seems to me not impossible that Avitus, who probably had some Gallic forbears, may reflect a Celtic curiosity about nature. The existence of such curiousity is, after all, testified to by an author as early as Julius Caesar, who wrote of the Druids: "Multa praeterea de sideribus atque eorum motu, de mundi ac terrarum magnitudune, de rerum natura, de deorum immortalium vi ac potestate disputant et iuventuti tradunt" (*De Bello Gallico* 6:14) ("What is more, they conduct many investigations and discussions of the stars and their motion, of the size of the earth and its lands, of the nature of the universe and of the strength and power of the gods, and they pass these things on to the young").

[8] On the pre-eminence of chastity as a tool for achieving sanctity, see Methodius, *Symposium* 10:1 (*P.G.* 18:191–94) 10:5–6 (*P.G.* 18:199–204), where he also presents the idea that chastity is taking control of mankind. See also Tertullian, *De exhortatione castitatis* (*P.L* 2:914ff.).

for grace, we can also glimpse in the text the psychological problems of adjustment and fulfillment that women must have faced in his own society.

It will be useful then, in examining the six poems of Avitus, to observe the interplay of these three related themes. We will first observe the manner in which he treats in verse the Christian vision of human history. He is among the earliest writers to undertake this task, probably the first, in a line that leads to Milton, to present in poetry a coherent overview of the entire Christian historical paradigm, an overview that includes an analysis of pre-lapsarian, post-lapsarian and redeemed mankind. This poetic undertaking necessarily implies a second, hermeneutical concern, for it is precisely that historical paradigm which will specify for him the significance of human acts. We shall, therefore, undertake as well a study of his handling of orthodox Christian hermeneutics and of his attitude toward the older philosophical and rhetorical traditions of his Greek and Roman predecessors and toward the intellectually unsophisticated pseudo-scientific impulses of his age. Third, we will trace a concern in Avitus' text with the moral valence of the physical world itself, noting in his treatment of matter a tension similar to that in his view of human understanding. We shall find on the one hand that, in keeping with his vision of human history, matter is often perceived as an impediment to spiritual achievement, nevermore so than when it is encountered as sexuality. At the same time, we shall discover in Avitus a poet's delight in the physical texture of the world and a curious fascination with the very sexuality he views as morally problematic.

*The Poems of Alcimus Ecdicius Avitus*

# The Poems

## *Prologue 1*

As we have noted, the first five poems of the collection are preceded by a brief prologue addressed to the poet's brother, Sidonius Apollinaris.[1] We are told in this prologue that it was in fact at his brother's urging that Avitus agreed to publish the five poems. Avitus had already published a collection of his sermons but, he reports, had lost most of his poetic works in what he refers to as "the well-known disturbances" of his age.[2] He then adds that he came upon the poems in the present collection among notebooks he had given to a friend and notes that the titles of the poems accurately describe their contents, in spite of the fact that the works also touch on other subjects, *alias tamen causas*, whenever the occasion presents itself, *inventa ... materiae opportunitate* (Prol. 1.1.14).

What does he mean by this statement? In all likelihood he is merely alerting his brother and other readers to the fact that his poems will contain a number of digressions from the central narrative, some of which present his own reflections on that narrative and provide both a running exegesis and occasional homiletic exhortations, others of which involve the embedding of subsidiary narratives, biblical, literary or historical, in the primary sequence of events.[3] Perhaps he sensed, in reread-

---

[1] An analysis of this prologue from the perspective of ancient rhetoric has been done by Roberts, "Prologue" 399–407.

[2] Probably related to the attack upon the Burgundians by Clovis in AD 500, Gregory, *Historia Francorum* 2:32–33 (*P.L.* 71:227–30). During this confrontation King Gundobad laid siege to Vienne and captured it.

[3] For a treatment of the various kinds of digression and a study of the number of lines in each book devoted to them as opposed to narrative, see Roncoroni, "L'epica biblica," 303–29.

ing his work, that his tendency to digress constituted a stylistic flaw. If this is the case, we have before us the first manifestation of Avitus' doubt about his ability to succeed in the composition of Christian poetry. As we shall see, Avitus never seems quite at ease as a poet. Even if we assume, as we must, that some of his reticence is formulaic and derives from a long tradition of self-deprecation in dedicatory prefaces, we cannot fail to see beneath this often mannered reluctance, real doubt about the viability of his poetic undertaking. For him the roles of teacher of doctrine and weaver of poetic diction and imagery are not easily wed. In fact, the digressions to which he refers constitute just a part of his elaboration and only a small portion of his paraphrase of the biblical narrative. Such an elaboration, especially in verse, must have seemed a challenging undertaking for a bishop, for he would, in attempting it, be going beyond mere exegesis, beyond a hymn's lyrical response to biblical narrative; he would instead be recasting the divinely inspired text in a medium perfected by the poets of pagan antiquity. A deeper reason for Avitus' lack of ease is then apparent, and apparent too is his own lack of confidence in his ability to carry out this enterprise successfully.[4]

As the prologue continues, Avitus reveals his self-doubt even more clearly. Poets who are not Christians, he admits, will question his inability or reluctance to employ the *licentia poetarum* which they claim. They will, therefore, brand his work as: "plus arduum quam fructuosum" ("more arduous than profitable"—Prol.1.2.8). It is not, then, simply a question of the stylistic or structural appropriateness of Avitus' elaboration. It is, as his own misgivings reveal, a question of whether he is undertaking a viable poetic task. Can the presentation of Christian doctrine and classical verse be successfully combined?

Avitus decided to try. He is, however, somewhat tentative and unsure of success. He makes his attempt with full knowledge of the difficulties it entails and takes care to distinguish between his practice and that of his classical models. He spells out clearly in the prologue the

---

[4] According to Michael Roberts, *The Jeweled Style* (Ithaca: Cornell Univ. Press, 1989), this kind of undertaking "presents late antique poetics in high relief, set off against the scriptural originals that underlie the poetic texts" (9–10). In other words, we can see clearly the poetic techniques employed by comparing works with scriptural archetypes. Roberts suggests that it is often the case that Christian poets accomplished this *poiesis* with ease: "Christian piety and secular literary preferences are woven together in a seamless web that manifests the unproblematic assimilation of these two traditions in the poet's own creative imagination" (146–47). This seems not entirely true of Avitus, as his prologue indicates.

ways in which Christian poetic narrative should differ from earlier Greek and Roman poetry. First, the form of the work must always be subordinated to the content: "salubrius dicenti clerico non impletur pompa quam regula et tutius artis pede quam veritatis vestigio claudicatur" ("For the cleric who is a poet works more good if he falls short in literary ostentation rather than in obedience to his rule of life, is safer if he lets his verse limp rather than fail to track the truth"—Prol.1.2.12). This separation of content and form is reinforced by Avitus' categorical rejection of content that is contrived, indeed, a rejection of all fiction or myth, which is regarded by him as falsehood: "quippe cum licentia mentiendi, quae pictoribus ac poetis aeque conceditur, satis procul a causarum serietate pellenda sit" ("Indeed, although a kind of freedom to tell false tales is granted equally to painters and poets, this freedom must be utterly banished from serious subject matter"—Prol.1.2.1–3). This formulation reveals the shift in mentality the Christian conception of history and the hermeneutic it fostered could achieve. For Avitus, the truth is now available to the Christian poet, and the significance of all events may be read in the cosmic vision presented in the scriptures. Fiction is no longer, therefore, a valid form of discourse for a poet who is concerned with the disclosing of eternal verities.

This confidence in the possession of the truth leads to a further restriction, one that strikes at the very heart of the poetic enterprise. Avitus suggests that the serious Christian poet should be wary of: "verba illa vel nomina, quae nobis nec in alienis quidem operibus frequentare, ne dicam in nostris conscribere licet: quae ad compendia poetarum aliud ex alio significantia plurimum valent" ("the words and terms which we ought not to dote on in the work of others let alone write in our own, which in the elliptical style of poets often carry now one significance, now another"—Prol.1.2.5–7). Avitus was obviously deeply troubled by the possibility that this kind of semantic and figurative ambiguity might be misused by the Christian poet. For him an open text in which metaphor produced multiple meanings represented a clear threat to the authoritative discourse of the Christian intellectual tradition.

Beneath these principles lies Avitus' strongest assumption: that poetry holds no privileged moral position. The Christian poet enjoys no license; he must operate within the discursive framework established by legitimate Christian authority. In short, the poetic word is to be judged by the same moral standards applied to all other words and acts.

Non enim est excusata perpetratione peccati libertas eloquii. Nam si pro omni verbo otioso, quod locuti fuerint homines, rationem redhibere cogentur, agnosci in promptu est illud periculosius laedere, quod tractatum atque meditatum, anteposita vivendi legibus loquendi lege, praesumitur. (Literary license is certainly not an excuse for the committing of sin. For if we assume that for every *idle* word that men have spoken, they must give a reckoning, it is clearly manifest that a poet's word, which has been carefully considered and employed, is fraught with greater spiritual danger and harm, if he assigns greater importance to the laws of speaking than to the laws of life.)          (Prol. 1.2.12–16)

The springs of Avitus' doubt in the face of the task of creating this kind of Christian verse narrative run deep. His anxiety is not merely stylistic or structural. He realizes, it appears, that he must attempt his poetic paraphrase in a literary context in which form must be rigidly subordinated to content, in which fiction and ambiguity are at least suspect and in which the rules of Christian *moralitas* take precedence over the rules of literary criticism. He appears to have some doubts about whether he can succeed, but he sets out nevertheless on a task that implies a serious revision in the canon of poetic literature, which will include poetic discourse wholly informed by Christian revelation of the truth.

## Poem 1

Avitus' first poem deals with creation and procreation and with mankind's use and abuse of the natural world. It begins and ends by focusing on sin and death, first retrospectively, then prospectively. At its very center the poet has placed a long and elaborate reference to the providential response to these dark forces, the redemption of humanity by Christ. The poem provides the reader with ample opportunity, therefore, to examine Avitus' treatment of the Christian view of history and of mankind's relation, intellectual and physical, to the natural world.

Avitus begins by attributing death to Adam and the sin he committed, thus distancing himself at once from the Pelagians, who believed that Adam injured only himself. This attribution is placed in a clearly procreational and hereditary context. Adam dooms his progeny with the seed of death *semine mortis* (1.7), and thereafter that progeny, which inherits the debt of death *debita leti* (1.11), incurs by its own actions a further guilt: "Addatur quamquam nostra *de* parte reatus" ("our own guilt plays its part as well"—1.5). This double guilt is not, however, the only theme of Avitus' opening stanza, for even in these opening lines the Redemption is foretold. He reminds his reader that "hoc totum Christus persolverit in se" ("Christ took all this on Himself and discharged it"—1.9), thus beginning his poem with a vision of the principal dramatic events that will mark his work: the temptation and fall of Adam and Eve, the continuing moral struggle of their descendants and Christ's redeeming act.

Having done this, Avitus turns to the act of divine creation and to the task of elaborating in 325 hexameters the content of the first two chapters of Genesis. The manner in which he achieves this elaboration needs to be carefully considered, for his technique provides further clues to his poetic sensibility and intellectual predisposition. At the very outset, for example, he employs a significant image, not used in Genesis, to describe the Creator's activity. God's command operates as a kind of cosmic balance: "omnipotens librantis pondere verbi" ("The almighty Father, creating equilibrium with His word alone"—1.14). Although God creates by word alone, a suggestion of physical instrumentality is inserted into the metaphor that signifies that act. What is more, the sequence of His acts is different from that in Genesis. In Avitus, the physical constituents of creation, water and earth, are mentioned first (1.15-16), whereas in Genesis (1.1-5), it is time that is first created by the separation of intangible elements, light and darkness. Indeed, for Avitus, time seems to spring from the movement of physical objects: the sun, moon and stars (1.20-23). Thus, although Avitus makes the Creator's mere will and word the shaping force of things, that force and its results are pictured in physical and even sexual terms: "et semen voluisse fuit" ("His mere willing of it was its seed"—1.27). With the creation of fishes, birds and animals yet another interest manifests itself, that in the mechanics of the creatures' bodies (1.30-40). The flying of birds and the ability of sea creatures to breathe under water attract the poet's interest, and this interest reveals in turn a curiosity about the variousness of nature and a sense that mankind errs in judging other creatures by its own categories. Nature is seen as greater than humanity and therefore worthy of contemplation on its own terms: "Quodque hominum falso credit mens nescia foedum, / Per propriam speciem natura iudice pulchrum est" ("What the ignorant mind of men mistakenly believes to be ugly, when seen for what it is, is beautiful in Nature's judgement"—1.42-43).

As Avitus turns to the creation of Adam, his poetry reveals the same interest in function and act. Indeed the Creator Himself, Who in Genesis creates man to till the earth, is here given a more abstract motive, an apparent delight in action for its own sake and a desire to observe movement and the dramatic change which human history will provide. God says: "Sed ne longa novam contristent otia terram, / Nunc homo formetur" ("To keep long inactivity from casting a gloom over this new earth, now let man be formed"—1.55–56). It appears that God wants history to begin and, like Avitus himself, will enjoy the elaboration of it by humankind. As He sets about the task of shaping man, He in fact reviews what the primary human occupations will be: the provision of physical sustenance through agriculture and, interestingly, the study and control of natural phenomena through the application of intelligence (1.60–68).

Avitus' description of the creation of the first human body can be read as a fifth-century lesson in rudimentary anatomy. Although he begins by comparing God to a sculptor (1.76–81), the poet soon abandons the image of an artist and undertakes an anatomical survey of the body by tracing the Creator's act. The parts of the body are generally described in terms of their function. The head's apertures provide sensation, the tongue, speech, the legs, locomotion and so on through the lungs, heart and other vital organs. As was the case in his description of animals, Avitus reveals the same fascination with the manner in which matter behaves. Remarkably, he goes on in the next stanza, contrary to the biblical account, to attribute life to the human engine before God breathes a soul into it: "Inde ubi perfectis consuescit vivere membris / Totus homo et fumant calefacta ut viscera, solam / Expectant animam" ("When the whole man grew used to being alive, with limbs now finished, as the body grew steamy with warmth, the soul alone was wanting"—1.121–23). In short, he sees the human body as capable of life without a soul and, when that soul is infused into it, it comes, as the double signification of the Latin *anima* itself suggests, as breath which man must draw in and nourish by physical inhalation: "quem protenus ille receptum / Attrahit et crebri discit spiraminis auras" ("And man, when he had caught the breath, at once drew it in and learned how to breathe regularly"—1.126–27).

Avitus then moves from the realm of bodily functions to the realm of human action in general. The Creator grants Adam dominion over the earth and its creatures, demands his obedience and service and adds a warning about worshipping images and empty gods: "Non species ullae nec numina vana colantur" ("Worship no other images or empty gods"—1.138). The Creator goes on to identify these: "Non si quid caelo sublime novumque coruscat, / Non quae vel terris vivunt formata vel undis / Nec quod forte premens prohibet natura videri. / Usibus ista tuis, non cultibus, esse memento" ("Nothing sublime or strange that may flash out in the sky, not the shapes that live on the earth or in the water, not that which Nature, by her own restrictions, may keep from sight. These are, remember, for your use not for your adoration"— 1.139-42). There is nothing unusual in the fact that the command forbids the worship of strange gods; what is curious, however, is that the phenomena listed are often objects of Avitus' own curiosity. Does he stand in danger of violating the very prohibition he is reporting? Probably not, but his interest does at times seem to contradict God's reminder that the world of natural phenomena is meant for mankind's *use* and that its study should, therefore, serve to answer humanity's legitimate needs, and not to satisfy its intellectual curiosity about the nature of things.

Avitus now turns from the creation of man and the natural world to the creation of Eve, who is formed, as in Genesis, from Adam's rib while he sleeps. Avitus notes that death as we know it was modeled on that sleep, drawing a somewhat ominous parallel, which he further develops by comparing the incarnation of Adam and Eve and the incarnation of Christ. Avitus then continues this figure by playing upon the wound caused by the removal of Adam's rib and the wound created by the Roman soldier's spear in the side of the crucified Christ. The blood of salvation issues from that second wound (as sin and death issued from the first?) and is augmented by the blood of martyrs, which, according to Avitus, is itself a figure signifying salvation. And the figure is taken one step further. As Eve rose from the rib of Adam, so the Church, Avitus reminds his reader, arose from the side of Christ as he slept in the tomb to be His bride.[5]

This complex figure is important, for it is the first example in Avitus' poetry of the use of the orthodox Christian hermeneutic which will inform his work. This interpretative approach is based upon the belief that while human history is linear, the significance of its contents, the events in that history, can be understood only by viewing it as a whole,

---

[5] The relation of the sacrament of marriage to Christ and the Church is dealt with early on by Methodius, *Symposium* 3:8 (*P.G.* 18:71–76).

by seeing it as God sees it, as a *totum simul*.[6] Viewed in this way, acts both human and divine assume the multi-levelled meaning that characterizes Avitus' poetry and later medieval thinking in general. Human history is a complex web of events figuratively related to one another and to the *veritas* whose consummation, although known prospectively through revelation, arrives only with the coming of the final moment, the *eschaton*.

We will need to be alert to the recurrence of figures of this kind and to their relationship to Avitus' partially suppressed interest in the observation of the natural world as an alternate interpretative tool. The dialectical relation of these two approaches to human understanding remains evident throughout the remainder of the first poem, in which Avitus describes first the institution of marriage and then the functioning of pre-lapsarian nature and the manner in which it is used by the first married couple.

As he returns to Adam and Eve, Avitus stresses the sacred nature of their relationship and the fact that it is a form of monogamous sexuality demanding fidelity. He refers to it as a *figura* (1.170), and we must assume that in doing so, he is again referring to the analogy of the human to the divine bride, the Church, as presented in the central figure discussed above. Marriage, as it is now established, is also seen as the means to achieving the linear extension of human history, the succession of generations that will provide the antidote to the *otium* or inactivity that was the cause of man's creation. In this pre-lapsarian world, however, the generations are, he explains, intended to coexist forever. The poet presents this intergenerational population explosion in an ingenious verbal arabesque: "Pronepos eductos spargens per saecla nepotes / Viventes numeret proavos inque ora parentum / Ducant annosos natorum pignora natos" ("May your great-grandson, scattering the offspring he has raised across the centuries, still number his own great-grandparents among the living, and may the offspring of his children lead their own children, themselves rich in years, before the eyes of their ancestors"— 1.177–79).

This theme of nature as it was originally intended, nature untouched by the Fall, occupies much of the poet's attention in the remainder of this poem. After the consummation of the marriage of Adam and Eve,

---

[6] This vision of history, its rise and its decline, is treated by C. A. Patrides in *The Phoenix and the Ladder* (Berkeley: Univ. of California Press, 1964).

Avitus presents a lengthy description of Eden, which, it should be noted, he sees as still existing in his own age, albeit inaccessible to mankind. This description is interesting because it reveals in two ways Avitus' curiosity about natural phenomena, as well as the manner in which he attempts to adapt that curiosity to Christian orthodoxy. First, the description of Eden is framed by two poetical treatises on geography. Having located Eden in the distant East, Avitus proceeds to consider that part of the world from an astronomical and climatological point of view, describing the negroid races which inhabit it, attributing their dark and, to him, repulsive skin to the climate, and finally touching upon the interaction between East and West in the form of trade in items such as ebony and ivory (1.193–210). After his description of Eden (1.211–59), he indulges in a second geographical excursus dealing with the four major rivers that flow from its spring (1.260–98). He identifies these as Tigris, Euphrates, Nile and Ganges and treats the last two in some detail.[7] In the case of the Nile we are given an analysis of the river's natural action, its ebb and flow, its remarkable fertilization of the land around it and the human adaptation to this phenomenon. In similar fashion the flow of the Ganges is described with a special view to its importance for human commercial activity.

Between these poetic treatises lies Avitus' lyrical description of Eden itself. It is perhaps one of the most beautifully executed passages in his poems and easily holds its own beside other utopian visions. It is wholly orthodox in that it presents nature as we would expect it to be in its pre-lapsarian form, free of flaw and without the marks of degeneration which the Fall will produce. Indeed, one is given the impression that this pre-lapsarian model of the natural world is being presented as a kind of Platonic ideal or archetype in contrast to which the reader may better understand the imperfect imitation of fallen nature.[8]

---

[7] The four rivers which spring from Eden's spring are frequently encountered in early Christian inscriptions and iconography. Their names are, for example, inscribed over a doorway in the early Christian church in Ostia, and they are also represented in the mosaic of the apse of the Church of St. Clement in Rome, a work which some believe may be traced back to the fourth century. These rivers also appear in other early biblical poets: Claudius Marius Victor, *Commentaria in Genesim* (also known as the *Alethia*) 1:270–304 (*P.L.* 61:944); Dracontius, *Carmen de Deo* 1:178 (*P.L.* 60:704).

[8] Curiously absent from Avitus' Eden is the tree of life of Genesis. As with so much of his revision, anything that tends to blur God's direct role in the Creation and ordering of nature, such as for example Adam's naming of woman and his specification of her role, are left out of his account. One wonders, as well, whether the tree of life may have suggested a form of idolatry not long suppressed in Avitus' culture.

The first poem concludes with the Creator's injunction that Adam and Eve not eat of the tree which: "Notitiam recti pravique in germine portans" ("Carries in its seed the knowledge of good and evil"—1.311). Significantly, he adds: "melius nescire beatis, / Quod quaesisse nocet" ("It is better for those who are blessed to be ignorant of what causes harm when it is examined"—1.314–15). Thus, as the poem draws to a close, two complementary notes are struck, the ominous naïveté of Adam and Eve, which will make them easy targets in the tragedy the second poem will present, and also a powerful doubt about intellectual curiosity which emphasizes the antithesis between happiness and potentially dangerous knowledge.

The structure of the first poem is by no means random. It opens and closes with references to sin and death. At its center lies the complex figure that treats Christ's redemptive act. This is framed by Avitus' treatment of the origins of sexuality and procreativity, the creation of woman, and by the institution of marriage; and these are in turn framed by two long passages, the earlier one on the creation of the natural world, the latter on the functioning of that world before the Fall. Avitus' structure is clearly graphic; it pictures the Christian cosmic vision as it might have been pictured in later centuries in stained glass. What is more, it shares with that medium both a delight in physicality and texture and in the illumination of these, in Avitus' case, through the application of the light of divine revelation and orthodox hermeneutics.[9]

## Poem 2

The story of the temptation of Adam and Eve, the subject of Avitus' second poem, is essentially dramatic. The introduction of conflict with the arrival of Satan inevitably produces a new dialectic of minds and wills, and so any treatment of the story, even in narrative form, will have a strong dramatic flavor. Furthermore, given the direction in which this dramatic episode moves, from ignorance to understanding, from moral light to darkness, from happiness to suffering and death, that treatment will be tragic as well. Not surprisingly, then, the structure of Avitus' second poem resembles that of tragedy, a structure in

---

[9] As Michael Roberts points out in his discussion of late antique poetics in *The Jeweled Style*, "The poetic text was understood in visual terms" (65). He prefers an analogy to mosaics (70), whose composition is, of course, not unlike that of stained glass.

which the actions and words of the three principals, Adam, Eve and
Satan, are punctuated by commentary both like and unlike that provid-
ed by tragic choruses. The commentary here is spoken by the poet him-
self and is based upon the specifically Christian vision of history dis-
cussed above. It serves to guide the reader's reactions in a more direct
manner than the choruses of Greek tragedy did, by reminding him of
the significance given to the events in the drama by that vision. It also
serves, as the Greek chorus often did, to transcend time and place, to
provide a retrospective and prospective view that enables the reader to
understand the events of the drama in the context of eternity.

The poem begins with precisely this kind of commentary. It serves
the purpose of bringing together the opposing wills in the drama: Adam
and Eve, whose present state in Eden is recapitulated (2.1-34), and Satan,
whose history and nature are given (2.35-117). It is not, however, the
characters alone who are presented in this opening section. We are also
introduced to the moral conditions and motivating forces, the anteced-
ent dispositions and impulses, that will drive the action. In the case of
Adam and Eve, for example, their integrity and freedom from physical
constraint and shame are emphasized, but there is an ambiguity, an un-
resolved contradiction in Avitus' explanation, and this constitutes the
first subtle indication of the moral danger that is to come. He states:
"Nam quaecumque bonus formavit membra creator, / Ut pudibunda
forent, carnis post compulit usus" ("Whatever bodily parts our benevo-
lent Creator formed, our flesh later caused to be filled with shame"—
2.23-24). The flesh is at least potentially a source of guilt and shame, and
by it Avitus clearly means human sexuality, as the following lines dem-
onstrate.[10] In these, the poet shifts his attention to the *eschaton* and to
the conditions of the blessed in Paradise. For them, he says: "neque
coniugium curae nec foedere turpi / Miscebit calidos carnalis copula
sexus" ("there will be no desire for marriage, nor will the joining of
flesh bring their passionate sexes together in a disgusting union"—2.29-
30).[11] Avitus then enumerates the major forms of human evil (2.31-33)
in a manner that suggests that all of them follow from lust, a lust which
in Paradise will be effaced by Christ, whose glory: "Sufficiet cunctis

---

[10] Augustine, however, in confuting the Manicheans, insists that there is no natural evil
in matter, *Civitas Dei* 11:23 (*P.L.* 41:336-37), and that sin is caused by the soul alone, *Civitas
Dei* 14:3 (*P.L.* 41:405-407).

[11] On sexuality in paradise, see Augustine, *Civitas Dei* 22:17 (*P.L.* 41:778-79) and Tertul-
lian, *Ad uxorem* 1:1 (*P.L.* 1:1274-77).

sanctorum" ("will answer the needs of all the saints"—2.34). Thus, the moral framework within which our drama will be played is also Platonic; sexuality is both a manifestation and a symptom of divine love. In the Christian view it is destined to be transformed into its divine source and end but, as the struggle in Eden suggests, that purpose may be subverted if sexuality, matter in its longing for its divine maker, falls under the spell of evil.

We are promptly introduced to that evil in the person of Satan. He is defined both by his history, which is given here, and by his present condition. The history of his fall demonstrates that his flaw was intellectual, that he lacked a full understanding of the divine plan. Indeed, Avitus is quick to point out that he felt himself autonomous, describing him as: "se semet fecisse putans" ("imagining that he had made himself"—2.40), and believing that he could achieve divinity through his own efforts: "'Divinum consequar,' inquit, /'Nomen et aeternam ponam super aethera sedem'" ("'I shall acquire,' he said, 'a name divine and shall establish my eternal abode higher than Heaven's vault'"—2.42–43). Avitus' Satan is portrayed as a creature in the clutches of a false consciousness that caused his fall from a position of preeminence among the angels. He remains a powerful being, but one who, deprived of the authentic identity his part in the divine plan provided, has now become essentially false.[12] Untrue to himself and to God, he can act only through deception. He will insinuate himself into matter and, in doing so, release the potential for evil that matter necessarily possesses as, in a sense, the underside of its longing for its divine destiny. Satan will become, Avitus tells us as his first commentary concludes, the active source of all human evil: "Nam quidquid toto dirum committitur orbe, / Iste docet scelerumque manus ac tela gubernat" ("Whatever dire deed is committed anywhere on earth, it is he who instructs the hand of crime and guides its weapons"—2.57–58). He is able to do this because: "futura videt rerumque arcana resignat" ("he sees the future and unlocks the secrets of the world"—2.54). In short, potentially evil flesh will now encounter an intellect, powerful but misguided, whose powers are capable of effecting its moral destruction.[13]

---

[12] On the character of Satan, compare Prudentius' treatment of the Fall: *Hamartigenia* 159–205 (*P.L.* 59:1023–27).

[13] For Boethius, however, evil is essentially powerless, in that it can never achieve true happiness. *De consolatione philosophiae* 4:2 (*P.L.* 63:791–96).

Satan now makes his appearance and, in a powerful monologue (2.89–116), provides the last ingredient required for the beginning of the dramatic action, his motivation for tempting Adam and Eve. This lies in his contempt for the newly created beings and in his jealousy, itself aggravated by his own recent loss. He senses that Adam and Eve are destined by God to replace him and his confederates, and in what becomes a vain attempt to avenge his own banishment, he decides to thwart the divine plan by making the hated creatures his companions rather than God's. Crucial to both Satan's motivation and his scheme is his awareness that God has determined that His new companions should be raised up from matter: "nunc ecce reiectus / Pellor et angelico limus succedit honori. / Caelum terra tenet vili conpage levata / Regnat humus" ("Behold, I am rejected and driven forth, and this clay succeeds to my angelic honors. Earth now possesses Heaven. The very soil, exalted in this base construction, now rules"—2.91–94).

The physical nature of Adam and Eve presents not only an affront, however, but an opportunity as well. Matter is weak, Satan understands, and may be seduced by beauty, especially if it is informed by falsehood. He therefore decides to make use of his adversaries' weakness and ignorance. The informing of matter by falsehood is aptly presented in Avitus' elaborate description of Satan's insinuation into the form of the snake (2.118–35). The snake's deadly weaponry, its phallic form and its long association with mysterious and even supernatural powers, render it particularly useful for the poet's purposes. It also provides an apt image of the lying intellect incorporated into a shining, seductive and yet frightening shape. The snake's contradictory image is emphasized in Avitus' simile of the snake awakening in the spring, which concludes with the chilling statement that: "Perfert terribilis metuendum forma decorem" ("His terrible shape bears a frightening beauty"—2.131).

The human couple are discovered already disposed to physical beauty, plucking apples from the trees of Eden. Satan doubts his ability to seduce Adam with his "firma mente virili" ("man's steadfast mind"— 2.140) and turns instead to Eve, here referred to as "Auditum facilem" ("the weaker ear" or "more easily seduced listener"—2.144). The suggestion that Eve's mind and flesh are weaker is interesting indeed, and we will have occasion to consider this further when we study Avitus' views on female sexuality. Here, however, it will be more profitable to concentrate upon the two primary tools used by the poet to delineate the scene of Eve's temptation: the subtle psychological study of Eve's reactions and the cosmic irony that envelops the entire scene.

These two devices are realized in the delicately balanced harmony of physical and intellectual temptations Satan presents. He begins with purely physical flattery but moves quickly to admiration of Eve's power over nature (2.145–56). Duplicitous from the outset, he denies that he is jealous and, all innocence, asks who has forbidden them to taste of the fruit of the tree of the knowledge of good and evil (2.157–60). Here, Avitus breaks into the narrative abruptly, chiding Eve for her lack of shame before an animal in possession of the power of speech (2.162–65). But Eve, who is described as "seductilis" ("open to seduction"—2.166), returns innocence for innocence and explains God's ordering of Eden in a pretty speech, finishing with a touching reference to death, which she asks the serpent to explain.

As Satan, now referred to as "leti magister" ("the teacher of death" —2.183),[14] responds, irony becomes more and more the vehicle that carries the meaning of the scene. The Christian reader of Avitus stood, of course, in a similar relation to the action of this narrative as did the Athenian audience to the action of a tragedy. As that audience generally knew something about the myth being treated and could read the action in terms of its fulfillment, so Avitus' reader sees the significance of this scene in terms of the *totum simul* of human history. He understands because of this privileged status the ignorance of Eve and the error of Satan. She has no knowledge of the death she will suffer; he, given his own experience, cannot understand death either. He does not entirely lie when he tells Eve that she will not die, for death and its significance will only be grasped through engagement in the divine plan as a participant in human history, something of which Satan is incapable.

Having won Eve's attention, Satan accomplishes her destruction by tempting her, as we have noted, with both intellectual and physical delights (2.166–227). In appealing to her vanity and intellectual pride, he suggests that the cosmos contains only two kinds of beings, animals and God. She and Adam, he explains, are being kept in the status of animals by a jealous Creator, Who keeps from them the secret knowledge that constitutes His divinity. The acquisition of that knowledge will confer divinity upon her and upon her spouse: "Namque hoc, quod vetitum formidas tangere, pomum / Scire dabit quaecumque pater secreta reponit" ("This fruit you fear to touch because it is forbidden will give you the knowledge of whatever your Father lays away as secret"—2.196–97).

---

[14] Prudentius has *magister mortis*, *Hamartigenia* 720 (*P.L.* 59:1062).

He adds at the conclusion of his lesson: "Mox purgata tuo facient te lumina visu / Aequiperare deos, sic sancta ut noxia nosse, / Inustum recto, falsum discernere vero" ("Your eyes will soon become clear and make your vision equal to that of gods, in knowing what is holy as well as what is evil, in distinguishing between right and wrong, truth and falsehood"—2.201-203).

Eve begins to waver, and Satan, seeing this, adds to the intellectual allure of divine knowledge the physical beauty of the apple, which he plucks and offers to her. Her reaction is utterly sensual and vividly described: "Sed capiens manibus pomum letale retractat. / Naribus interdum labiisque patentibus ultro, / Iungit et ignorans ludit de morte futura" ("She took the deadly apple from him and held it in her hand. Without further prompting she brought it to her flared nostrils and parted lips, as in her ignorance she played with the death that was to come"—2.214-16). The climax arrives and Avitus skillfully describes Eve's internal struggle. Her mind moves among four points, arranged as two polarities: the apple and death, intellectual pride and God's law. Stage villain to the end, Satan holds the apple before her eyes, complains about her hesitation and, as she bites it, continues his dissimulation by concealing his joy (2.233-38).

The reader, appreciating the irony of Avitus' description, understands that in terms of the divine plan both Eve and Satan are misguided. She will in fact die and his victory will in fact be undone. But the dramatic tension is maintained, for the poet introduces Adam at once, a naïve, almost comic Adam, coming fatefully in search of Eve's embraces and kisses,[15] seeking a spouse whom he will find no longer innocent, himself predisposed therefore, to temptation and compliance (2.235-37). Eve rushes to meet him, and it is at once clear that she will be her husband's Satan. Her guile recalls the serpent's as she appeals to his male vanity and, with what Avitus calls her "femineos furores" ("female madness"—2.239), boasts of her own daring. Adam sins at once, "constanter inconstans" ("firm in his infirmity"—2.259), having displayed no signs of the mental struggle that preceded Eve's fall.

The scene ends with a pyrotechnic piece of stage business, the ap-

---

[15] It is interesting to note here that, according to Augustine, Adam and Eve engaged in sexual intercourse but experienced no lust before their fall, *Civitas Dei* 14:23 (*P.L.* 41:430-32). Dracontius has Adam experience *affectus novos* when he first catches sight of Eve, *Carmen de Deo* 1:392 (*P.L.* 60:729), but whether lust is signified we cannot tell. Curiously, Avitus uses the same phrase of Adam and Eve as they first experience remorse (3.210).

pearance of a strange and mournful light around Adam's face, a light accompanied by what Avitus calls "novos visus" ("strange visions"— 2.264). We are witnessing, Avitus tells us, the origin of blindness. And yet, the reader cannot fail to judge that Adam's *peripeteia* and *anagnorisis* are at heart Sophoclean, for his fall has come with the acquisition of a horrifying knowledge. Adam, like the Sophoclean hero, can now see within himself and recognize in actuality the evil that had been in his flesh only potentially until it was impregnated with Satan's false consciousness.

This momentous act and its moral and mental implications elicit from Avitus a long commentary on human curiosity and counterfeit knowledge (2.277–407). It is divided into two parts, one dealing with the desire to know what is hidden and therefore illicit, a category typified by the future, and a second dealing with curiosity about evil itself as manifested in human history. In the first part of this commentary, Avitus submits as types of human longing for illicit knowledge both the Egyptian magicians who vainly imitated the wonders worked by Moses and the Marsian snake charmers.[16] The reference to Moses' confrontation at the Egyptian court is interesting because it foreshadows Avitus' more extensive treatment of this scene in the fifth poem and also because the miracle and magic depend upon the transformation of a rod into a snake. The phallic image of the snake, recently presented as the embodiment of Satan's false wisdom, will in fact be featured in both parts of this commentary. In each section, however, the snakes typify a different kind of false wisdom. The Egyptian magicians imitate God's miracle, arrogating to themselves a knowledge of the hidden and transformable nature of matter only the Divinity should possess. Their knowledge constitutes a kind of illicit capability to perform miracles. The Marsians, on the other hand, attempt to know what is hidden by time, i.e., the future, which they learn of, they imagine, by conversing with the dead. Both they and the Egyptians are deluded. God overpowers the magicians' portents and sends the Marsians answers to their questions that are without significance. Avitus concludes this condemnation of curiosity about what is hidden with these words: "Praesenti inlusus damnabitur ille perenni / Iudicio, quisquis vetitum cognoscere temptat" ("Whoever attempts to understand what is forbidden will be made a

---

[16] On the misguided and illicit use of magic and astrology, see Sidonius Apollinaris, *Carmina* 5:129–32 (*P.L.* 58:662) and Augustine, *Civitas Dei* 5:1–7 (*P.L.* 41:139–48).

mockery of today and condemned by a judgement that is eternal—2.324–25).

He turns next to the second form of illicit curiosity, that which seeks to know human evil. Here he selects the wife of Lot as his example, (Gn. 19.24–36) a selection that serves several purposes. First, it enables him to picture for his reader the extreme forms of human degradation the Fall he has just described would in time produce. It also foreshadows the principal theme of his fourth poem, human defiance of law and its punishment. Finally, and most significantly, both Eve and Lot's wife typify for him female susceptibility to temptation, although their susceptibility differs in several ways. The motivation of Lot's wife is baser, little more than a kind of voyeurism. Eve's sin is intellectual pride reinforced by an attraction to physical beauty. Most important, Avitus reminds his reader, Lot's wife does not become the teacher of the evil knowledge she gains; her significance is communicated only through the very form of her punishment. In the passage in which the poet describes the woman's transformation into a pillar of salt, he instructs us in the manner in which she will signify in the future. Playing on the connotations of the word "salt," he describes her as: "quae pungere sensus / Exemplique potest salibus condire videntes" ("she who can sting our senses and preserve with the salt of her example those who see her"—2.398–99).

The length of this commentary and the consequent hiatus in the dramatic movement of the poem may appear at first to be a structural flaw, and indeed the three principal characters do recede from the reader's view during this lengthy digression. In making such a judgement, however, we risk foisting on late antique sensibilities an earlier classical ideal.[17] It is important to keep in mind that the drama that elicits Avitus' greatest concern is the great drama extending from the Creation to the Last Judgement. An historical consciousness of this kind, when coupled with the obligations of a cleric-poet, as adumbrated in the first prologue, required the inclusion of just this kind of didactic, exegetical dimension in even the most dramatic text, and, the more significant the action of the drama, the more elaborate is the commentary required.

Avitus' drama of the Fall, in some ways a prototypical mystery play

---

[17] Roberts, *The Jeweled Style*, makes a similar point: "Poetry of the period [late antiquity] is often described as episodic, but what is involved is no more than the application of the principle of *variatio* to large units of composition." He further notes: "Late antique poetry has its own unity, but it is conceptual and transcends the immediate historical content of the narrative" (56–57).

that attempts to dramatize Christian discourse, ends with a powerful so-
liloquy (2.408–23). As the poem draws to a close, Satan takes the center
of the stage once again to boast of his victory. His analysis of the dra-
matic outcome, although flawed in a way he cannot understand, is mas-
terly. His victory, he proclaims, is an intellectual victory. He has
opened to mankind knowledge of what is hidden. He has worked a kind
of cognitive revolution in God's creation that has revealed and actual-
ized evil, an evil he wrongly imagines will triumph eternally. Thus Avi-
tus has him proclaim: "Quod docui, meum est; maior mihi portio restat.
/ Multa creatori debetis, plura magistro" ("What I taught is mine, and
the greater portion remains with me. You owe much to your Creator
but more to your teacher"—2.420–21).[18] And so, with a philosopher's
boast he vanishes in a cloud of smoke.

## Poem 3

The themes of Avitus' third poem are divine judgement and redemp-
tion and mankind's response to both sin and grace. The poem has an ex-
traordinarily complex structure, which presents a cosmic history of
these themes, beginning with the judgement of Adam and Eve and ex-
tending to the Last Judgement. It builds upon several complex figures,
draws widely from biblical parables and includes echoes of what may be
events and attitudes that marked the poet's own age.

We discover Adam and Eve in the evening of the day of their Fall,
afflicted by its first effects. It is a sexual reaction, the sense of shame at
their own nakedness, that first troubles them, and we see them taking
steps to deal with it by seeking clothing (3.1–19). This image of clothing
will recur frequently in the poem, signifying in different ways the now
fallen, vulnerable and degenerate nature of humanity. Here, for example,
the rudimentary clothing of the first couple signifies their depravity and
makes it manifest: "nudumque malum de veste patescat" ("[they] lay
bare their wickedness by wearing clothes"—3.11).

---

[18] Echoed by Milton, *Paradise Lost* (New York: Odyssey Press, 1935) 4:110–13, as Mer-
ritt Hughs has noted. The question of whether Milton knew Avitus has been discussed by
Daniel J. Nodes in *Avitus: The Fall of Man* (Toronto, 1985). He notes the strikingly similar
characterization of Satan and the verbal stylistic parallels between the two poems. These
similarities and the fact that Avitus' poem was not only known (first edition 1507) but even
used as a text in grammar schools in the seventeenth century, suggests that Milton may well
have read Avitus early in life.

Their search for clothing in the form of foliage from the trees of
Eden is linked to an even more complex figure, which is so important
it needs to be quoted in full:

> Et tamen adveniet tempus, cum crimina ligni
> Per lignum sanet purgetque novissimus Adam
> Materiamque ipsam faciat medicamina vitae:
> Qua Mors invaluit, leto delebere letum.
> Aereus excelso pendebit stipite serpens,
> Cumque venenantum simulaverit, omne venenum
> Purget et antiquum perimat sua forma draconem.

(And yet the time will come when a new Adam will heal and
cleanse the sin of one tree by means of yet another tree, when he
will make that same substance a medicine of life and, Death, just
as you once grew strong, so then you will be destroyed by death.
A brazen serpent will one day hang from another lofty branch
and, although seemingly poisoned, will wash away all poison and
destroy the ancient snake with its own form).        (3.20–26)

This figure links the Fall and Judgement with the Redemption of
mankind. The tree in Eden provided the apple by which Adam and Eve
were seduced, and a nearby fig tree provided the leaves that signify their
guilt. The tree on which Christ will hang will provide life, as the tree of
the knowledge of good and evil provided death, and Christ, a brazen ser-
pent like that of Moses (John 3.14) will be raised up, overcoming and
destroying the Satanic snake.

Having established in this figure the link between Fall and Redemp-
tion, Avitus further explores the reactions of Adam and Eve to their
new state (3.27–40). Their actions continue to reveal a desire to hide, to
conceal themselves and indeed to escape shame through death itself,
whose nature they do not yet fully comprehend. When this desire over-
takes them, Avitus pauses to comment upon it and upon the relation-
ship between their first step in sin and their final step on earth, that to-
ward the grave. He uses this observation on the relationship between sin
and death to extend the historical perspective of the poem by painting
two more scenes of death and judgement, the punishment of Sodom in
the post-lapsarian age and the Last Judgement itself (3.40–65). Thus,
within the first sixty-five lines of the poem, Avitus relates the Fall to the
entire expanse of human history, and in doing so, emphasizes the com-
mon moral status of all mankind in its relation to sin and grace.

The appearance of the Creator further provokes the fallen couple's desire to hide and engage in deceit (3.66–80). Now as false as their seducer, they contrive pathetic excuses for their flight, revealing at once their own depravity by confessing their sense of sexual shame. Clothing and nakedness provide the key image for their first exchange with their Maker after the Fall. God Himself sees the significance of their shame at once and proclaims: "Hactenus et nudis nunc denudata patescunt, / Arguit obscenus quia turpia corpora motus" ("To that extent the nakedness presents itself to the naked, because a disgusting urge tries to prove your bodies foul"—3.88–89).

The first trial in human history then begins with the cross-questioning of Adam and Eve by their Creator (3.81–115). The defense of the criminal pair is wretched and cowardly. Adam blames his wife[19] and God as well for having created the instrument of his fall. But if he suggests that God was indirectly his seducer, Eve at once blames the serpent, and so, when the sentence is pronounced, it contains a triple verdict, as in Genesis (3.14–19), directed toward the serpent, Adam and Eve. Each creature receives a special judgement, but the three of them are linked to one another (3.116–94). The snake's doom includes not only his physically abject and eternally terrifying image in the eyes of mankind, but also the curious prediction, also made in Genesis, of his relation to Eve and her descendants: "Semina seminibus mandent ut vota nocendi. / Insistens semper pavidae sectabere calcem: / Conterat illa caput victoremque ultima vincat" ("Seed will commit to seed the promise of revenge. You will always wait stubbornly upon the frightened woman's heel and I decree that she will at last crush your head and overcome the one who overcame her"—3.134–36). Avitus, following the orthodox Christian exegesis of the narrative in Genesis, is quick to note that the final words of this sentence constitute the first signification of Christ's incarnation.

As the serpent's punishment is linked to Eve's, so her punishment is linked to Adam's, for it is the subjection of woman to her mate that will lie at the heart of her future suffering. It is significant that, for Avitus,

---

[19] The reader will note that Avitus' construction of the character of Eve in these three poems is based on her being "other." Adam, God and Satan are all male; they are adversaries but share a common understanding. Eve is different, both weaker and mysterious. Here (3.110–15), even the Divinity accepts Adam's cowardly shifting of the blame to this strange outsider.

this subjection is essentially sexual and vile and that procreation is viewed, in this post-lapsarian context at least, as a "naturale malum" ("a natural evil" or "nature's own curse"—3.147). The production of a child is characterized as a "poena parentis" ("a parent's punishment"—3.148), a characterization to which we shall return when considering Avitus' attitude toward sexuality and procreation in his last poem. Adam's punishment, on the other hand, is related not to procreation but to the maintenance of life, to the provision of sustenance through gruelling work. It is extended first by Avitus to the very nature of human nourishment and to the inevitable decay of the body it implies and then to the evils inherent in social and economic intercourse, the anger and violence that will follow the human struggle to survive. Especially evident in this description of Adam's fate, as we will see in later sections of this poem, is the reversal of the image of the benign pre-lapsarian nature found in the description of Eden in the first poem. Very possibly there are also echoes in these passages of Avitus' own experience of the decline of cultivation and social order in his own day.[20]

Far from having made themselves superior to the beasts, as Satan had promised, Adam now leads a life that is ironically: "aequalem brutis" ("like that of the beasts"—3.170).[21] God Himself provides him and his mate with clothing, significantly, in view of their changed natures, the skins of animals, and drives them from Eden (3.195–219). With their judgement completed, they quickly grasp the horror of their new condition, first physically, then intellectually, as they take in the world around them, and finally emotionally, as they experience remorse for the first time. Remorse is for them: "adfectus novos" ("a new emotion" —3.210), but one Avitus recognizes as an essential ingredient in the evolving economy of redemption. It is not surprising, therefore, that he pauses to analyze this concept, emphasizing the fact that its efficacy is time-bound, that to achieve salvation the sinner's remorse must occur during his earthly life. So important does Avitus consider this lesson that he places at the very center of this poem a surprisingly long version of the parable of Dives and Lazarus (Lk. 16.19–31), in which Dives, the rich man, is the type of sinner whose remorse comes too late (3.220–

---

[20] Gregory mentions a pestilence that attacked central Gaul in AD 464, *Historia Francorum* 2:18 (*P.L.* 71:215–16) as well as a famine among the Burgundians during the episcopate of Sidonius Apollinaris, *Historia Francorum* 2:24 (*P.L.* 71:220–21).

[21] Similarly, Augustine notes that, in trying to become more, man became less, *Civitas Dei* 14:13 (*P.L.* 41:420–22).

310). This long narrative section not only vividly defines the role of re-
morse in determining the fate of the individual sinner, it also picks up
several other dominant motifs in the poem. Clothing and nakedness are
significant images within it, as are human nourishment and bodily
decay. The judgement of Dives echoes the judgement of Adam and Eve,
and the great chasm between Lazarus' heaven and Dives' Hell recalls the
distinctions between Eden and the dreadful world into which the fallen
couple flee.

Indeed, this entire episode has a decidedly topographical character.
The Christian view of history, treated until now in primarily temporal
terms, is now presented in a spatial perspective. Earth, Heaven and Hell
are developed as geographical correlatives of the three moral conditions
possible for human beings after the Fall: the struggle for salvation on
earth, blessedness in Heaven, damnation in Hell. What is more, these
places are characterized by an antithetical equation that demonstrates
that an abundance of illusory wealth on earth leads to real poverty in
Hell, just as the temporary poverty of the living is reversed by their
abundant life in Heaven. Thus Avitus describes Dives as a man: "Quem
nimio luxu dissolvens vita fovebat" ("whom life pampered as it de-
stroyed him with too much luxury"—3.221), and he has a somewhat
vindictive Abraham say to the doomed Dives: "uterque / Permutate
vices: et te iam sufficit amplis / Exundasse bonis, laetetur fine malorum
/ Qui doluit coeptis" ("I order each of you to suffer a reversal of fates.
As for you, be satisfied now that you enjoyed a superfluity of wealth
then, and let him who grieved over his original state take joy in the end
of his woes"—3.288–91). Orthodox topology and temporality intersect
precisely at the point Avitus emphasizes at the conclusion of the narra-
tive. The time and space of earth are morally undetermined, open to
grace and the workings of the human will. The map of Heaven and Hell
is, as the parable teaches, a map of morally closed places where the des-
tinies of their inhabitants are forever fixed.[22] This is graphically dem-
onstrated by the most chilling topographical detail, given here by the pa-
triarch: "Insuper horrendo currit qui tramite limes / Et chaos obiectum
lato distinguit hiatu, / Non sinit abiunctas misceri foedere partes"
("Rather, a boundary that runs around a frightening track and cuts off

---

[22] Prudentius is less severe. He tells us that the damned are given a holiday once a year
to mark Christ's resurrection, *Liber Cathemerinon* 5:125–36 (*P.L.* 59:827–29). On the other
hand, Dracontius, *Carmen de Deo* 3:64 (*P.L.* 60:843) insists upon the same *immane chaos* be-
tween Heaven and Hell.

the chaos opposite us with a wide chasm, does not permit the joining of
places separated by divine covenant"—3.292-94).

Having given his reader a vision of cosmic topography, Avitus turns
his attention back to the post-lapsarian landscape in which Adam and
Eve find themselves. He does not linger, however, over the condition of
the couple themselves. Instead, he further traces the degeneration of na-
ture, introducing the now violent behavior of animals and making an
easy step from that to the violent behavior of men (3.333-61). In short,
Avitus gives us here a preview of evil in history, the evil of natural ca-
tastrophe that nature inflicts on mankind and the evil that humanity
works upon itself. He is preparing his reader in this preview for the fol-
lowing poem that will present the darkest hour of ante-diluvian deprav-
ity. It is worth noting that while physical violence and war are given
places in this prospectus, along with the role they play in producing
sudden reversals in human fortune, legal quarrels and litigiousness are
even more prominent. To some degree this may reflect Avitus' own so-
ciety. It also provides in this poem about judgement an ingenious anti-
thesis between the justice of divine judgement and the flawed jurispru-
dence of humanity, for human legal proceedings, the imperfect replica
of what the reader has witnessed in this poem, are in fact little more
than surrogates for warfare in Avitus' view: "At si forte brevi re-
quiescant tempore bella, / Legibus armatas furere in certamina lites, /
Ius anceps pugnare foro?" ("And if it happens that there is a lull in the
warfare for a short time, need I mention that suits armed with laws
foment wild contention, that ambiguous legal claims do battle in the
courts?"—3.348-50).

At the beginning of this poem, Avitus linked the Fall and the Judge-
ment of Adam and Eve to the Redemption achieved through the Cruci-
fixion of the second Adam. He accomplished this through the elaborate
metaphorical scheme based upon the two trees, the tree of the knowl-
edge of good and evil and the tree of the cross. As he brings his poem to
a close, he returns to the theme of the salvation of mankind. This theme
is now treated in contemporary terms, from the perspective of Avitus'
own age. It is couched in an elaborate prayer on behalf of the Christian
community, whose salvation still hangs in the balance. The prayer is one
of Avitus' most complex structures. It is constructed around two sets of
triplets, each of which contains three metaphorical representations of
Christ's redemptive act. The first three figures are given in rapid succes-
sion and constitute a kind of overture to the prayer (3.362-70). They
present the Redeemer as the potter who mends the broken vessel, as the

finder of the lost drachma and finally as the shepherd who brings home the lost sheep. The order is obviously incremental: a common object is restored, a valued object is rediscovered, a creature is restored to its flock.

In the second triplet the biblical *exempla* are more fully developed, are linked to the predominant imagery of the third poem and are punctuated by theological commentary which reveals Avitus' anti-Pelagian stance by stressing the helplessness of the figures in each tale and their total dependence on assistance, i.e., grace. Once again, they are arranged in a climactic order that takes us from an event distant from the act of Redemption to the Crucifixion of Christ itself. Avitus first treats the parable of the prodigal son (Lk. 15.11–32). He tells the story briefly but fully (3.370–83), playing upon the imagery of food and clothing that have played so important a role earlier in the poem. He then employs the image of the son's garment in the intricate theological elaboration of the prayer that follows (3.384–95). Noting that, unlike the father of the prodigal son, God suffers no loss through human sin, Avitus prays that God will change the tattered cloak worn by humanity after the Fall for His finest garment, presumably that of salvation.

The second parable in the triplet is the story of the good Samaritan (Lk. 10.29–37), whose actions are attributed here to Christ Himself, Who saves all sinners as the Samaritan saved the traveller attacked by thieves and abandoned on the road (3.396–406). This figurative expansion of the significance of the parable provides the basis for the prayer that follows (3.407–408). In the preceding prayer, Avitus asked for the garment of salvation; in this prayer he asks for the oil of grace, which will heal the sinner's wounds and lead him to the protection of the Samaritan's inn, given here as a figure for Paradise.

In these first two members of the triplet Avitus has metaphorically elaborated the act of salvation, first by characterizing it as the replacement of a torn garment, then by comparing the bestowal of grace to the gift of healing oil in the transformed tale of the Samaritan. In the third member he presents directly, without metaphor, the actual achieving of blessedness. Here he employs the story of the thief on the cross beside Christ (Lk. 23.40–43), who typifies for him the faithful Christian who actually achieves Heaven. As crafted by Avitus (3.409–23), the account recapitulates many of the earlier motifs of the poem. The thief's wretched condition, like that of Lazarus, is illusory. He leaps to Paradise, reversing the fall of Adam and Eve and traversing the topography described in the Dives narrative. Most important, Avitus achieves closure by returning to the image of the tree of the Crucifixion and to the countervailing force it brings to bear on fallen humanity in the economy of divine grace. Avitus ends his prayer: "Livida quos hostis paradiso depulit ira, / Fortior antiquae reddat tua gratia sedi" ("May Your even more powerful grace return to their ancient seat those whom the jealous anger of their foe drove from Paradise"—3.424-25), and in doing so, repeats the antithesis presented at the beginning of the poem: Fall: Anger; Grace: Salvation.

## Poem 4

This poem contains Avitus' description of primitive or, in biblical terms, ante-diluvian mankind. It presents a vision of the deterioration of the earth and its creatures, a deterioration, which we are told, continued after the expulsion of Adam and Eve from Eden. All of the consequences of sin were not, Avitus affirms, realized at once. Indeed, that realization is revealed in this poem as a process that characterizes the early period of human history. It leads to two events: a reversal of God's creative act through the Flood's destruction and the introduction of the notion of an elect people who will be redeemed in time and preserved in the interim in a divinely ordained structure that looks back to Eden and forward to the Church. Avitus' fourth poem is an account of the manner in which the Divinity achieves these two things. Beneath its surface, however, lie two significant problems of treatment, both of which merit our further consideration.

First, since he is now dealing with early human history, Avitus must take into account the pertinent views of the Greeks and Romans and either refute or explain them. Since he is also dealing with the history of the Hebrew people, he must at the same time incorporate into his text a revisionist exegesis of the Old Testament narrative.[23] Second, since he will be once again elaborating the contents of just a few chapters of Genesis (6–9), and since those chapters contain matter that is bound to stir his curiosity about both nature and mankind's technological response to natural catastrophe, he has to strike a balance in his descriptive passages between curiosity and artistic elaboration on the one hand and the orthodox view of these events as symbols of divine will on the

---

[23] In discussing Old Testament paraphrase Reinhart Herzog, *Die Bibelepik der lateinischen Spätantike*, notes that Israel is no longer viewed as simply the historical nation but as "die Kontinuität des auserwahlten Volks in einem christlichen Geschichtshorizont" ("the continuation of the chosen people on a Christian historical horizon" [114]).

other. To accomplish this Avitus emphasizes the unnatural or miraculous in his elaborate description of the Flood and the direct role played by the Divinity and his messenger Gabriel in the design of the ark. He is also careful to include in his text an explicit condemnation of the arrogant misuse of technology in the tale of Babel and its tower.

It is true, of course, that the problems Avitus faced in shaping his paraphrase were shared by many other Christian authors, especially by poets such as Juvencus, Sedulius and Claudius Marius Victorius who produced biblical paraphrases. On the other hand Avitus' poetic sensibility, as explained in his first prologue, surely makes the task of accommodation more difficult. As Kartschoke has noted,[24] in Avitus we find a new stage in poetic consciousness, a consciousness that, one must conclude, considerably complicated his task.

Avitus begins with a broadside attack on the Greek version of primitive history as represented by the Deucalion legend, which he brands as a: "fabula mendax" ("false tale"—4.3), whose author was not, as he is, "veri compos" ("in possession of the truth"—4.8). Having claimed this high ground, Avitus spends nearly the first quarter of the poem describing the condition of early humanity (4.11–132). The human race's further degeneration is identified at once as the logical consequence of Adam and Eve's sin: "propria valuit pro lege voluntas. / Ius adeo nullum" ("his own will assumed the power of law for each individual. Indeed there was no notion of justice"—4.13–14). In this passage Avitus emphasizes humanity's inheritance of Satan's false autonomy, and to this rejection of law he attributes the rise of violence and bloodshed in beasts and in human beings, all of which leads to a licentiousness so excessive that he refuses to describe it in what he calls his "casto cantu" ("unsullied song"—4.31).

After a brief reference to the ironic metamorphosis of the first man and woman from creatures made in God's image to beasts, Avitus traces the course of humanity's decline in two lengthy similes, one of which describes the lapse of untended fields into unkempt woodland (4.37–54), the other, the course of a stream of water which grows in time into a raging torrent that carries all before it (4.62–75). The similes are complementary. The first, possibly drawn from Avitus' own experience of the decline of agriculture in his troubled age, pictures decline in its slow, almost imperceptible stages. The second, the image of the river, notes the

---

[24] Kartschoke, *Bibeldichtung*, 72.

modest beginning of motion but then emphasizes its rapid growth and eventual overwhelming power.

To these similes Avitus adds further historical details, among them the extraordinary length of human life in the period he is describing. Nor is he satisfied with the mere reporting of this biblical information. He analyzes it and concludes that longevity itself and the great distance to which it removed death were factors in the decline of human morality. They were not, however, the only factors. Avitus appears to believe that a kind of biological degeneration occurred as well and that it produced the race of giants referred to in Genesis (6.1–4). Not only does he affirm that such a race existed but he goes on to describe it in some detail (4.86–93). He must reject, of course, what he considers the outrageous elaboration of the giants' history by Greek poets, along with the Greek myth of the piling of mountains on top of one another in an attempt to reach the sky (4.113), but even this rejection permits him to comment upon a similar transgression, the building of towers with the same intent. The story of tower building in the tale of the tower of Babel is, of course, accepted as true, and his reference to it enables Avitus to include in his narrative the accompanying story of the multiplication of languages, the basis, in his view, of the very existence of the varying historical traditions with which he is struggling.[25]

The following reference to languages and their role in guiding human curiosity and the technology it spawns is revealing:

> Hinc sparsum foedus, scissa sic lege loquendi
> Consensum scelerum turbata superbia rupit,
> Dum se quisque suis, possit quae noscere, verbis
> Adgregat atque novas sequitur gens quaeque loquellas

(For this reason, when the laws of language were torn apart, the builders' confused arrogance dashed to bits the criminal compact they had agreed to. Each person joined the group whose words he could understand and each nation adopted a new tongue.)

(4.123–26)

---

[25] For Augustine's treatment of the multiplication and diversity of languages, see *Civitas Dei* 16:4 (*P.L.* 41:482–83) and 19:7 (*P.L.* 41:633–34). Nor is Avitus alone among the poets in his interest in the nature and use of language. This concern also is found in Dracontius, *Carmen de Deo* 3:627–32 (*P.L.* 60:894–95), who seems to view language more as a signifier of mentality than as a tool for communication and control. Thus he refers to it as *interpres mentis, secreti pectoris index,* and *cordis imago.*

What are we being told here? First, there are, in Avitus' view, enterprises that go beyond mankind's legitimate need to sustain itself and are, therefore, illicit by nature. Second, language, which is capable of abetting such enterprises, should not be misused in such a way. And finally, the multiplication of languages and consequently of literatures and cultures is, in Avitus' view, a means by which God curtails such illicit intellectual curiosity and activity. Ironically, in the light of this formulation, Avitus' own linguistic undertaking may be seen as a reversal of the original fragmentation of languages and cultures, an activity that makes available to his readers truths concealed in an inaccessible text, but that, in so doing, also runs the constant risk of exceeding the legitimate bounds of human curiosity.[26]

In the second quarter of the poem, Avitus turns to the reaction of God to the decline in human morality. Avitus' Divinity seems in this passage to be curiously, unorthodoxly, anthropomorphized. He grieves, hesitates and displays in a long soliloquy an unbecoming and vengeful wrath. It is, in short, an almost human Father who decides at last to reverse His act of creation by restoring the world to its ancient state: "Ad chaos antiquum species mundana recurrat/Inque suas redeant undarum pondera sedes" ("Let the appearance of the earth rush back to ancient chaos, let mountains of waves return to their former places"—4.160–61). It is almost as if God had not understood the power of Satan and sin, as if His exile of Adam and Eve from Eden had proved, surprisingly even to Him, an insufficient punishment. Now, all of creation must be destroyed, at least for a time. The natural reversal that followed mankind's fall will be repeated on a cosmic scale.

There will be, however, one exception, as there must be if Satan is not to triumph. One man, Noah, and his family will be spared and will become the second source of the race.[27] This selection introduces a new element into the historical vision Avitus is presenting. The fallen race will be neither totally doomed as were Satan and his band, nor totally redeemed. There will exist within the race an elect group, a group,

---

[26] Early Christian thinkers concerned themselves with the status even of translations of scripture. Augustine suggests that the translators who produced the Septuagint were in fact guided in their work by the Holy Spirit, *Civitas Dei* 18:43 (P.L. 41:603–604).

[27] An analysis of the story of Noah and its reception by Christian critics may be found in Don Cameron Allen's *The Legend of Noah* (Champaign: Illinois Univ. Press, 1963).

we now learn, which will be initiated by Noah, who will gather his family into the ark, the vehicle of escape from universal destruction. Avitus presents this notion of an "elect" very carefully, conscious, one imagines, of the possible injustice suggested by it. He takes pains to stress Noah's unique piety and traces his illustrious lineage and descent from Enoch (4.172-89), all of which justify his selection and provide a precedent for special divine favors.

If the image of God is humanized as He reacts to evil on earth, He is more remote in His dealing with Noah in Avitus' narrative than in the biblical story. In Genesis God speaks to Noah directly, but here He sends the archangel Gabriel to deliver His message. Why, one wonders, did Avitus, after giving God a soliloquy of grief and wrath, feel the need of an angelic intermediary? God loses the speech which He delivers in Genesis and in its place Avitus places Gabriel's speech of over fifty lines (4.227-82). It is not unlikely that Avitus' narrative strategy simply reflects a great interest in angelic beings among early Christian authors.[28] But there may also be further reasons intrinsic to the text. The nature and work of angels is carefully described, and Gabriel's pre-eminence, his role in the Incarnation for example, is emphasized (4.190-212). It is more likely that we are dealing with a carefully planned antithesis. Gabriel is the reverse image of Satan, the successor to his honors. As Satan seemed the instrument for denying God's plan, Gabriel is in fact the instrument for achieving it. There is a nice dramatic symmetry in this. Satan's fall prepares for the creation of mankind but then subverts it temporarily; Gabriel prepares for man's redemption here and finally plays a crucial role in achieving it. He represents, then, the moral and historical antithesis of Satan's misguided and false autonomy.

The use of the archangel Gabriel may have been prompted by other considerations as well. It permits Avitus to include a long, detailed set of technical instructions to Noah, something he may have felt would have been inappropriate on the lips of God Himself. It also provides the occasion for the spectacular arrival and departure of the resplendent creature,

---

[28] Augustine deals with both angels and demons in *Civitas Dei* 9-12 (*P.L.* 41:255-376) *passim*. A similar delight in angelic appearances is evident in other early Christian poets, e.g., Juvencus, *Evangelicae Historiae* 1.46, 1.87, 1.195, 4.747 (*P.L.* 19:64, 70, 85, 341). On the other hand, Claudius Marius Victor, *Commentaria in Genesim* 2 (*P.L.* 61:953-54) follows Genesis and has God speak directly to Noah. It is also possible, of course, that the practice of biblical poets also reflects the practice of classical epic poets, who frequently employ divine intermediaries like Hermes and Iris.

thus giving the poet an opportunity to indulge his fascination with flight of all kinds.[29]

Gabriel's message includes two kinds of information. He reveals God's plans for universal destruction and God's selection of Noah as the vehicle for preserving the race. He then gives Noah specific instructions for the achievement of this end. The ark is described and its passengers are carefully listed. The vessel will be a second Eden. In it animals will be tame and obedient and, as in Eden, Gabriel warns, only the serpent will have to be carefully watched. He warns Noah: "Hic semper suspectus erit penitusque cavendum est" ("[He] will always be suspect and must be watched with the greatest care"—4.280).

Avitus' treatment of the preparation of the ark, which occupies the next part of the poem (4.293–428), is in fact an extended figure in which the ark signifies the bulwark of salvation the just prepare in the expectation of the final judgement and in which the reactions of Noah's contemporaries signify the foolhardiness of doomed sinners.[30] The entire situation surrounding the ark's construction is treated as a foreshadowing of the end of the world. Hence the actual building of the ark is dealt with in a mere twelve lines (4.293–305), most of them devoted to the felling of trees on mountains drawn, interestingly, from Greek myth. Much more attention is paid to the reactions of the crowd as it watches the construction. Indeed, its scepticism is, in a curious way, a reflection of the tension in the poet's own mind. Its members manifest the same curiosity about physical phenomena and their laws he sometimes manifests and they quite correctly judge that the ship will never, as long as the natural laws of physics hold true, be set afloat. Avitus is quick to point out, however, that these rational and empirically based calculations are false (4.311). His criticism follows logically from his own assumptions about the significance of natural phenomena. In fact, although nature follows certain rules in most cases, this is not what is important about its processes.[31] The real significance of natural phe-

---

[29] A frequent metaphor, the flight of birds is described at 1.32–34, 4.546–52 and 4.565–84. Angelic flight occurs here and at 6.596–602. The flight of Elijah in his chariot is described at 4.178–84.

[30] For both Gregory, *Historia Francorum* 1:4 (*P.L.* 71:164) and Augustine, *Civitas Dei* 15:26 (*P.L.* 41:472), the ark is the type of the Church.

[31] One finds a very different attitude in Boethius who has Philosophy remark: "cum naturae tecum secreta rimarer" (when with you [Boethius himself] I would scrutinize the secrets of nature), *De consolatione philosophiae* 1:4. 14–15 (*P.L.* 63:615). Avitus' attitude here tends to support Marrou, who, as we have noted, finds that late antique interest in natural

nomena lies in their use by the Divinity to reveal His plan and to bring
it to fulfillment. However fascinating the workings of the physical
world may be, humanity errs in making its laws its main concern. The
reaction of Noah's audience is typical, Avitus explains, of the distracted
modern thinker who reads nature incorrectly. The result of this is con-
flict and confusion: "Haut aliter studium iam tunc diviserat omnes, /
Quam nunc mundus habet" ("Their conflicting enthusiasms divided all
of them, just as the world's distractions take hold of us now"—4.318–
19). Avitus adds that this confusion afflicts even those who read nature's
text correctly, who realize that the end of the world is approaching:
"qui ... operi rebusque instare supremum / Discrimen norunt, corpus
quo concidat omne" ("who know the final peril that closes in on the
world, that peril in which all that is corporeal will crumble"—4.319–21).
Concern for the physical world, for understanding, manipulating and
enjoying it, is a distraction that leads to the moral blindness which
Avitus here catalogues. As modern sinners call the just foolish, so the
crowd around the ark brand Noah insane, and, as the mocking crowd
around Noah will be destroyed, so too God will destroy sinners when
Doomsday arrives.

Avitus further elaborates this figure as he turns to the loading of the
ark (4.344–428). A keen observer of nature still, he notes that the ani-
mals have a premonition of the coming of danger which the human ob-
servers lack. This observation gives him the opportunity to explore fur-
ther the nature of intellectual blindness and its interference with the
essential human contribution to the negotiation of salvation, remorse.
Avitus demonstrates this by giving two historical parallels: the fates of
Sodom and Nineveh—the first utterly demolished by God's wrath, as we
saw in the preceding poem, the second saved by remorse and repentance
(4.355–90).

The story of Nineveh also permits Avitus to introduce the story of
Jonah (4.358–87) and to provide, as he does so, two additional insights
into the attitudes of his contemporaries toward repentance. First, the
role of a prophet is explained. He is an individual who is able to read
the text of the natural world correctly, discovering in it the accomplish-
ment of the divine plan. The prophet then uses this reading of events to

---

phenomena often focuses on the marvelous and unusual in its attempt to "établir que la
réalité est extraordinaire," *Saint Augustin*, 156, and therefore, we must assume, capable of
being used by God to work his own ends.

overcome his listeners' blindness and distraction and to produce in them the requisite remorse and repentance. Second, the form which that repentance takes in Avitus' lesson is the rejection of the world and the adoption of the asceticism and self-denial that attracted Christians in his age and that would characterize medieval monasticism in the centuries to come.

As Noah's family enters the ark, Avitus permits himself a brief digression on the origin of slavery (4.404–17), including in his text the biblical story of Ham's being given to his brothers as a slave because he had dared to look upon his father naked (Gn. 9.20–25). Why this digression? Avitus may have judged that his readers would wonder about slavery and human bondage and whether it existed in this early period. In fact, there are other indications in the poems that in his own age men were reduced to bondage as a result of indebtedness. More important, however, is the fact that Ham's punishment is the result of an illicit curiosity and that the poet explicitly draws a comparison between physical slavery and bondage to sin. In short, the story of Ham resonates with the very theme we have been tracing: the relation of illicit curiosity to moral blindness and bondage to depravity.

The description of the flood itself (4.429–584), both the waxing and waning of the waters, moves on two levels, literal and figurative. The literal level is a poetic *tour de force*, rich in vivid imagery, compelling action and strong emotion. And beneath these artistic "hydro-technics" one can discern the same fascination with natural processes, even when events are produced by divine *fiat*. The descriptions are dazzling poetry, but a rudimentary scientific curiosity lingers there too.[32] For example, Avitus' curiosity about the nature of precipitation is apparent. He understands the phenomenon of evaporation but seems also to hold to the theory of the massive and organic subterranean circulation of water (4.446–47). Such received ideas fetter his empirical instincts, not least of all the notion found in Genesis, that the order of nature is based upon the separation of elements: earth, water and sky—a concept that lies beneath much of the poet's imagery. As a result, his natural speculation is

---

[32] It is important to remember that for the ancients science and poetry were not rigidly separated categories. In presenting scientific ideas in verse, Avitus places himself in a tradition that stretches back to Manilius, Lucretius, and even the pre-Socratic philosophers.

often a mixture of valid insight and error. In discussing the nature of the rainbow, for example, he demonstrates an understanding of the passage of light through moisture: "Pendulus obliquum solem cum senserit umor" ("When the pendent moisture felt the sun passing through it"— 4.627), but the source of the colors in the bow he can attribute only to the various elements from which he suggests they are drawn, the sun, the clouds and the earth. Beyond that he senses only a vague harmony in the phenomenon, a "*concordantia*" (4.635) whose cause lies for him in the supernatural realm, whose effect is understood in poetic and moral, not empirical, terms.

As always, Avitus' curiosity about natural phenomena gives way to the orthodox hermeneutic of Christianity. As the waters rise and grow more violent, the ark is assailed by their fury and tossed about by the waves. Avitus draws the obvious comparison. This vessel of salvation is like the Church, which is assailed by storms in a similar way (4.493–501). The threats to the Church are, however, intellectual, he tells us, assigning them to four agents: the pagan barbarians, the pompous wisdom "*turgida sapientia*" (4.498) of the Greeks and Romans, the *charybdis* (4.497) of heresy[33] and finally, what is called the raving voice "*rabido ore*" (4.496) of Judaea. These intellectual currents which assail the Christian community represent for Avitus false readings of the text of nature and of history, and they lead to a kind of intellectual intransigence. This becomes clear as the simile of the ark is extended. As the ship is naturally buoyant and yields to the buffeting of the sea, so the Christian, the poet insists, must yield, intellectually one assumes, to the mysteries of the cosmos (4.506–9).

In the directory of the misguided the Jews occupy a special place and are singled out later in the poem for special chastisement. When the seas begin to recede, Noah sends birds from the ark, hoping that they will return with indications of the condition of the outside world (4.563–84). One of these, a crow, is distracted by the carnage on the earth and never returns. Avitus compares his behavior with that of the Jews in his own day, of whom he says: "Sic nescis, Iudaee, fidem servare magistro, / Sic carnem dimissus amas, sic gratia numquam / Custodi vitae dominoque rependitur ulla" ("Jew, this is like your ignorance of how to keep faith

---

[33] Prudentius, on a similar note, refers to heresy as *discordia, Psychomachia* 709 (*P.L.* 60:72).

with your Lord. Although freed by Him, you too love the flesh in this way and render no thanks to the Protector and Lord of your life"— 4.569–71). This is an interesting commentary, when taken together with the reference above, on early anti-Semitism. It suggests that the basis of such feeling was largely a kind of intellectual and moral exasperation and insecurity.[34] The Jew is a scandal for Avitus above all because he persists in refusing to allow the incorporation of his scripture and tradition into the framework of Christian orthodoxy. He does not, in short, accept the discursive authority of the Church and the historical vision it propounds. As a result, he remains attached to the world and involved in its natural and social processes in a way that seems perverse to a Christian bishop for whom Doomsday is imminent. The Jew represents for Avitus a special subcategory of the unrepentant and deceived, special because in his view the Jew should logically stand among the elect, and special as well because his intellectual intransigence presents a unique challenge to orthodoxy.

Avitus closes his fourth poem by addressing the attitudes of the faithful who are disposed to salvation. Using the rainbow of God's pledge as his starting point, he constructs an exhortation which, although homiletic in form, contains a figurative matrix that recapitulates the major motifs of the poem (4.621–58). He explains to the faithful: "Illud suspicies signum, quod signa figurant" ("You will look to that sign which other signs represent figuratively"—4.640). The sign is, of course, Christ. The rainbow is not only a sign of God's promise not to destroy the world again by flood; it also signifies Christ, the central and pre-eminently meaningful sign, in that, like Him, it is a mediator between heaven and earth, partaking of the nature of both. And, since He issues a pledge to mankind only those washed by baptism can accept, the flood itself is, therefore, another sign that represents the baptism of the redeemed. Even the redeemed, however, must earn Christ's gift by cherishing it in their lives, and so Avitus' extended figure concludes with the suggestion that salvation must be lodged in an ark that will protect it from the guilt and death that the water of baptism has washed away. In

---

[34] For the attitude of Sidonius Apollinaris to the Jews, see *Epistolae* 6:11 (*P.L.* 58:559–60). On the question of their perceived intellectual stubbornness, see also Methodius, *Symposium* 9:1 (*P.G.* 18:173–79). Gregory, *Historia Francorum* 5:11 (*P.L.* 71:325–26) gives an account of a particularly violent outbreak of anti-Semitism in AD 576, in which a later bishop of Clermont, also named Avitus, was involved. The same sense of exasperation with what was seen as Jewish intellectual intransigence marks the event.

his final lines, he in fact reverses the impact of God's promise never to destroy mankind by water by reminding his reader of the final peril, the fires of Hell. The gift of salvation must be cherished, he warns: "Ne post ablutum valeant discrimina crimen: / Et flammam timeas, quo iam non suppetit unda" ("So that after your guilt has been washed away, spiritual perils do not regain their strength, that you need not fear the flames, in that place where water now brings no aid"—4.657-58).

## Poem 5

The story of the Jews' exodus from Egypt lends itself naturally to epic treatment, and so it is not surprising that Avitus' fifth poem, which deals with this event, has the form of a miniature epic. Focused on the making of a nation, it has all the hallmarks of a national saga and resembles in many ways Vergil's great Roman epic, echoes of which are not infrequent in the text.[35] The Hebrew nation is hardened and shaped by wandering and suffering. A leader emerges and receives special supernatural guidance. An enemy people, seemingly more powerful and advanced in civilization, must be overcome. Divine portents and supernatural interventions occur, and preparations for battle are extensively described. Special attention is also given to the emerging nation's culture, especially its religious rituals, and the text is marked by a decidedly moral tone, which glorifies the behavior of the victors and condemns the offenses of their enemies. If the *Aeneid* is about the making of Romans, Exodus is about the making of the Jewish people.

Avitus is, therefore, employing and revising two earlier literary traditions in this poem. He must accommodate the biblical story of Exodus to the Christian cosmic vision and also reshape classical epic structures and devices to make them serve as a vehicle for that revised story. In tracing the course of his narrative, it will be useful to observe how these traditions and the requirements of orthodoxy are reconciled.

Two principles soon become apparent. First, on the moral and eschatological level, fundamental changes in both the Hebrew and Graeco-Roman narrative strategies will be made. Supernatural forces in Avitus' poem will be far more directly and spectacularly involved than in class-

---

[35] For a thorough treatment of this, see Michael Roberts, "Rhetoric and Poetic Imitation," 29-70.

ical epic. At the same time, the moral tenor of the poem will be carried by the same typology that we have found in the earlier poems, a typology generated by the Christian view of history. Second, from the standpoint of narrative technique, the Graeco-Roman model will prevail. The movement of the narrative and its elaboration through speeches, as well as much of the diction, will follow the classical models, to which occasional didactic and homiletic passages will be added.

Avitus begins the poem with an expression of his ambivalence toward the value of mere poetic achievement (5.1–18). He repeats his belief that the poet does not occupy a privileged position and that the reader's response in the form of moral edification is of primary importance. This edification is achieved, he notes, not by the: "dignum eloquium" ("the grace of style it [the story] deserves"—5.6–7), but through the realization that the story: "Causarum mage pignus erat pulchramque relatu / Pulchrior exuperat praemissae forma salutis. / Historiis quae magna satis maiorque figuris" ("represented more than anything a pledge of things to come, and the nature of the salvation it promised surpassed in beauty the beauty of the narrative. The work's beauty was great enough for the story it told but still greater in the figurative sense"—5.15–17). In short, the reader is put on notice that Avitus intends to use classical poetic techniques, not as mere ornaments, but to teach the true significance of the scriptural account of the Exodus. He will perform an exegesis of the Old Testament text with classical poetic tools.

Avitus takes up his narrative with the confrontation between Moses and the Pharaoh, spending only a few lines on the history of the Jews' sojourn in Egypt and on Moses' colloquy with God at the burning bush (5.19–97). Nevertheless, this backward glance, however brief, permits him to introduce several important motifs: the hardening and growth of the Jewish nation, the cruelty of the Egyptians, and the dramatic intervention of the Lord. All of these themes are further developed in the scene at the Pharaoh's court, the most dramatic features of which are the metamorphosis of Moses' rod into a snake and the contest between him and the court magicians that follows (5.62–97). The scene is significant because it introduces the central motif of the poem, the reversal of natural law by the Divinity and His agents. The reader recalls, of course, that a similar reversal occurred in the fourth poem, and in fact Avitus announces at the beginning of this poem that his theme will be a natural reversal which is the very opposite of the one he has just dealt with, i.e., land will now overcome water instead of water overcoming land.

This direct and elemental intervention by supernatural forces is one of the ways in which Avitus differs from his classical models. Vergil's gods are permitted to influence and use natural events but they cannot overturn natural law itself.[36] In the classical epic, fundamental modification of nature or natural behavior is more likely to follow from human effort, as is the case with Aeneas' descent into the underworld. For Avitus, it is precisely this kind of elemental tampering by man that is wrong, just as here, in his first scene, the Egyptian magicians are seen as wrong. We encounter again Avitus' orthodox view of the limits and uses of human knowledge. In this poem, more than ever, it becomes clear that the manipulation of the physical universe is a power reserved to God, Who uses it to signify His plans and to carry them out.

Although Avitus diverges from his classical models in his treatment of supernatural intervention, it is the classical norm to which he adheres in adapting the biblical narrative. In keeping with the need to present a single recognizable epic hero, the role of Aaron is virtually eliminated in Avitus' rendering of the story, and attention is focused on the confrontation between two individuals, the hero Moses and the evil Egyptian leader. If there is any deviation from the epic usage, it lies in the characterization of the Pharaoh, who seems throughout the poem something of a stage tyrant, petulant, even childish, less impressive than the cold and hard-hearted adversary in the scriptural account.

Avitus' treatment of the subsequent plagues with which God punished the stubborn Pharaoh (5.127–217) is strikingly different from the biblical account (Ex. 7.14–10.30). The nature of the afflictions is virtually the same, but the manner in which they are described and the organization and pace of the narrative are much altered. The biblical account achieves its effect by the accumulation of parallel incidents in which the actions of the Divinity, Moses and Aaron respond to the actions of the Pharaoh and, in the earlier episodes, to the actions of the court magicians. The descriptions of the plagues themselves are pithy and spare. The narrative is concentrated upon the contest of wills as the same conflict is repeated again and again in almost the same pattern. The power of the narrative springs from this very repetition, from the very same-

---

[36] The storm which Neptune and Juno stir up in *Aeneid* I is violent but not unnatural. Unnatural phenomena such as the turning of Aeneas' ships into nymphs (10.220) are more properly viewed as mere poetic devices or fancies, not as serious commentaries upon the relation between Vergil's gods and natural law.

ness of action, which demonstrates forcefully both the Pharaoh's intransigence and the determination of God to save His people.

Avitus, in following the narrative patterns of classical epic, alters the biblical approach to the story of the plagues. Moses and Aaron are both removed from these episodes. There are no human confrontations; God produces the plagues and the Pharaoh reacts. The emphasis is upon the description of the plagues themselves and upon the psychological effects they produced. What we find in Avitus' text is a rhetorical but naturalistic elaboration of the scripture's spare description, an elaboration driven once again by the poet's unfailing interest in natural phenomena and human psychology.

A few examples will demonstrate the mingling of rhetorical techniques with this interest in matter and mind. Here is Avitus' description of the fiery hailstorm:

> Ignibus inseritur praegrandis pondere grando,
> Non ut nube solet terris nimbosa venire:
> Sed quemcumque cadens ut deprimat atque ruinam
> Pondere vel solo faciat. Coniungitur ergo
> Grandineum flammis ferventibus aere frigus. . . .

(Hail of great weight was mixed with fire and fell to earth, not in a storm cloud as is normal but in chunks capable of crushing and bringing destruction to each victim with their impact alone. The iciness of the hail was joined in the air with seething flames. . . .)           (5.186–90)

As for Avitus' interest in psychology, it is sometimes germane to the action, sometimes peripheral to it. He says of the Egyptian's reaction to the plague of boils and fever: "Creditur hic etiam casu contingere languor: / Sed morbus mentis discrimina corporis urget" ("Even this weakness, however, they believed had overtaken them by chance, while, in fact, the disease of their minds was causing bodily peril"—5.179–80). Here the self-delusion of the Egyptians is essential to the action, but in some passages Avitus' acute observation produces a distracting, pedestrian and even comic effect less appropriate to the epic style. Of the swarms of gnats he observes: "Et licet immersis defigant vulnera rostris, / Plus horror quam poena movet" ("and although they inflicted wounds with bites, fear of them agitated men more than the actual punishment they inflicted"—5.168–69).

In the more spectacular reversals of nature the rhetorical texture grows richer. Here is Avitus' description of the dark night that enveloped Egypt:

> Squalentes pariter viventia milia credas
> Infernas intrasse domos aut forte revulsa
> Obice terrarum patriam sordentis abyssi
> Migrasse in superos ac mundum luce fugata
> Sub leges misisse suas.

(You would have thought that a thousand creatures had entered the murky halls of the dead together or that by chance the barrier of the earth's surface had been pulled away, that the land of the foul abyss had shifted to the realms above it and that, with light gone, had subjected the world to its own laws.)

(5.210–14)

Even here, however, the imagery is accompanied by a homely reference to the chemistry of firebuilding: "et si sopitos flando quis suscitet ignes / Aut flammas excire velit, compressa necantur / Lumina nec vibrant restrictos pondere motus" ("If anyone had a mind to rouse smoldering fires by blowing upon them or wanted to stir the flames, the fire's light was extinguished and died. Nor did it unfurl tongues of fire, muffled as these were by the weight of the foul atmosphere"—5.205–207).

The central portion of the fifth poem (5.218–356) contains an account of the institution of the feast of the Passover, the destruction of the Egyptians' first-born, and their decision to release the Jews and assist them in their departure. Predictably, the Passover is given significance beyond that which it has in the Old Testament account. Presented as a sign of God's choice of the Hebrew people, as a means to that nation's salvation, and a manifestation of the people's acceptance of their special status as the elect of God, it recalls the sacrifices made by Noah after the flood when he and his family were constituted an elect people. But Avitus also adapts this ceremonial to the specifically Christian perspective of his poem. For him, the Passover prefigures Christ's redeeming act and the Christian liturgy that re-enacts it. Furthermore, Avitus' treatment of the figure through which he accomplishes this adaptation is complex, and the congruences it inscribes are somewhat curious. Christ is seen as the lamb sacrificed to save the elect from death, but the sign placed on the forehead of His people is not the sign of blood but of baptism: "Sic nos, Christe, tuum salvet super omnia signum / Frontibus impositum" ("As Your sign, Christ, when it is placed on our foreheads, is our best salvation"—5.247-48). The significance of this for Avitus' readers is clarified in the further elaboration of the figure:

> Tu, cognosce tuam salvanda in plebe figuram
> Ut, quocumque loco mitis mactabitur agnus
> Atque cibo sanctum porrexerit hostia corpus
> Rite sacrum celebrent vitae promissa sequentes.
> Fermento nequam duplici de corde revulso
> Sincerum nitidae conspergant azyma mentis

(Understand, reader, the special meaning and significance of this for you, living as you are among a people marked for salvation. Henceforth, in whatever place the gentle lamb is sacrificed and the victim provides His holy body as food, let those who abide by His promises of life fittingly perform their own holy ceremony. Plucking from their false hearts yeast without value, let them sprinkle around the true leaven of a radiant mind.)    (5.254-59)

The emphasis is liturgical. As the slaughtered Passover lamb signifies Christ, so the Passover ceremonials signify the re-enactment of His sacrifice in the Mass. Finally, as a cap to this figure, Avitus draws a new comparison, employing God's instructions concerning the consumption of unleavened bread (5.258-59). But the simile must now take a new turn. The image of eating has already been exhausted, and so the field of the figure is moved to the hearts and minds of the celebrants. The simile ends on a moral note: the Christian, now saved by Christ's sacrifice, must rid himself of the world's false yeast and cultivate an unleavened (ascetic?) mentality (1 Cor. 5.7-8).

The arrival of the angel of death is simply but movingly described: "Ecce venit tacito per dira silentia motu / Angelus, exerto missus qui saeviat ense" ("And, behold, with quiet tread, the angel came through the ominous silence, he who had been sent by God to wreak havoc with his drawn blade"—5.267-68). He accomplishes his grim work, slaying the Egyptian first-born with an impartiality that gives Avitus an opportunity to reflect upon the even-handedness of death and on its inability to efface the good deeds of the just. There are echoes of Lazarus' story here and of Noah's, but these are not made explicit by the poet, who turns instead to the reactions of the Egyptian people to the slaughter. These fall into three stages. First, their grief is portrayed (5.291-307).

Avitus' description of it is capped by a vision of the unburied dead, which is so vivid that it suggests that he may have drawn it from his own experience.[37] Then the Egyptian people rise up against the Pharaoh, acknowledging the Jews' supernatural protection and urging their release (5.308–31). Finally, confessing his defeat, the Pharaoh agrees to allow the Jews to depart (5.331–70).

Once again, the motif of reversal, of the Divinity's power to turn the natural course of events around, is stressed. Here, however, the reversal is not merely physical, as was the case with the earlier plagues; it extends to the minds and hearts of the Egyptians, eventually accomplishing acts of generosity which run entirely counter to the expected patterns of human behavior. Avitus comments, as he brings this episode to a close, on the fact that this kind of reversal is commonly worked by God: "Nonnumquam rectis et, quae contraria, prosunt / Et, quae laeva malus voluit, mutata recurrunt / In dextrum vertente deo" ("Sometimes what seems misfortune works to the advantage of the just, and what an evil man wishes to be a curse is changed by God's blessing into a blessing"—5.352–54). In short, God's interference with the laws of nature, an extraordinary event on the physical level, is even more common, according to Avitus, on the moral level, a view that foreshadows his description of his own age in the final poem. There, the precariousness of life and the frequent reversals of fortune seem to discourage the human engagement of evil and to promote a dependence on the kind of divine disposition of affairs suggested here.

Reversal continues to be the dominant theme in the second half of the poem. The Jews, long captive in the land of Egypt, are now driven from it by their former masters, who are themselves destroyed by the climactic reversal of natural laws in the Red Sea. Like the second half of the *Aeneid*, the second half of this miniature epic is a battle narrative.[38] There is, however, an important difference. All of the trappings of battle and all of the rhetorical armory of battle narrative are present, but no battle occurs. Appropriately, the reversal of fortune is accomplished entirely by the Lord, once again through His reversal of natural law.

The epic narrative that follows is, therefore, suffused with a profound irony. The brilliant descriptions of the two armies are not pre-

---

[37] In addition to calamities already noted, we may note Sidonius Apollinaris' comments on the condition of Gaul, *Carmina* 5:356–63 (*P.L.* 58:669).

[38] Roberts, "Rhetoric and Poetic Imitation," has carefully analyzed Avitus' adaptation of the narrative and rhetorical techniques of Vergil and other earlier Latin poets.

ludes to their clash. They serve rather to heighten the reader's awareness of their ineffectiveness. The ultimately fantastical nature of the military preparations of both people is foreshadowed several times in the narrative and is underlined most strikingly by the image of the pillar of fire God sends to be the protector of the Jewish nation. Indeed, after describing both the military and civilian components of the Jewish horde, Avitus is careful to point out: "Sed non haec acies acie salvabere ferri" ("And yet, the edge of your battleline was not to be saved by the blade's edge"—5.391), but rather: "Unus pugnabit cunctis pro milibus auctor" ("Their Author alone would fight on behalf of all those thousands of men"—5.393).

Avitus' description of the pillar (5.401–49) recalls his description of the rainbow in the fourth poem. We discover in it the same rhetorical elaboration, the same underlying interest in natural processes, even here, where natural reversal is involved. The natural course of events may be supernaturally altered, but the poet nevertheless describes the effects of the pillar on the night sky with a physicist's eye: "Diffugiunt tenebrae vicinaque sidera cedunt / Et latuit rutilis oppressus fulgor in astris" ("The dark shadows departed, the closer stars gave way and their glitter, once it was effaced, lay hidden among the ruddier constellations"—5.410–11). Thus, although Avitus bases his rhetorical treatment of the pillar on the notion of similarity in difference, he remains an observer of nature as well. What is more, the description of the cloud's protection of the Jewish nation during the daylight hours suggests the sensibility of not only an artist and scientist but a technician as well.

The account of the Hebrews' journey abounds in images of God's assistance, of the nation's initial awe and eventual grateful acceptance of this aid. The protection and guidance of the pillar is the most striking example but other examples follow: the miraculous endurance of their garments (5.452–55), the manna from Heaven (5.456–61) and the water drawn from the rock (5.462–66). The final examples receive figurative development: the manna, which is sent from Heaven for man's spiritual nourishment, is said to signify Christ's body, a kind of "pascenda salus" ("meal of salvation"—5.460), and the water and rock from which it is drawn are similarly presented as signifying Christ as a "stabilem petram" ("hard rock"—5.464), which, when struck, "Porrexit suis sacro de vulnere potum" ("provides drink for His people from His wound"—(5.466).

Attention is focused upon the Egyptians as the poet resumes the account of the rekindled conflict between the two nations (5.467). His narrative is punctuated by a series of seven speeches, a set of three leading to the final confrontation and presenting the states of mind of the antagonists, another pair of speeches at the climax of the conflict reflecting dissension among the Egyptians, and a final pair at the resolution of the action, one by God instructing Moses to close the sea, and one by the Pharaoh confessing his defeat.

The subject of these speeches can in fact be reduced to a single issue: can there be a meaningful and effective military contest between the two human armies at this moment in history, at this point in the text of divine providence? The first speech, delivered by the Pharaoh, argues that the Egyptians were in fact deluded in their belief that human conflict should be avoided (5.472–96). Avitus has him draw an interesting sociological and economic picture of his country's decline after the departure of the Jews. The poet then describes in considerable technical detail the arming of the obviously superior Egyptian army. The sophisticated and terrifying armor of the Egyptians frightens the Hebrew people and also heightens the irony inherent in the narrative.[39] Avitus reminds his reader of this even as he turns to the account of the Hebrews terror: "itur ad unam, / Quae claudat cunctas pelago pandente, ruinam" ("they [the Egyptians] were destined for a single destruction, which would close upon all of them as the sea spread open"—5.542–43).

The Jews do, however, despair, and the final speeches in the first set of three contain their lamentation (5.547–53) and the speech of encouragement delivered by the nation's priests Moses and Aaron (5.558–74). In the end the Jews' fear that armed conflict will break out is put to rest by their own leaders' statement of how the resolution of the conflict is destined to occur. While they are not permitted, as the poet is, to know the manner in which the Divinity will intervene, they are confident that intervention will take place: "caeli pugnabitur ira, / Qua vobis placido peragentur praelia nutu" ("the wrath of Heaven will have to be contended with. With it and with nothing more than an untroubled nod from the Lord your battle tomorrow will be concluded"—5.573–74).

As the final day dawns, Avitus moves the Hebrew nation to the edge of the Red Sea, whose parting has been accomplished by God, not in fact with a simple nod, but through the application of hot dry winds. Once again, the result of this climatologically produced reversal of nature is described by the poet with a technician's eye: "Machina, pen-

---

[39] Contrast Sidonius Apollinaris' description of the Huns, the appearance of whose bodies and faces is more terrifying than their armor, *Carmina* 2:245ff. (*P.L.* 58:649).

dentis struxit quam scaena liquoris, / Frenatas celso suspenderat aere lymphas" ("A structure, which a wall of hanging water had created, held the sea back and kept it suspended in the air"—5.592–93). Having described this technical marvel, he moves the fleeing nation through the gap it has provided, pausing to note, even in this climactic moment, the lengthening of the sun's rays, which now must struggle to reach down to the floor of the sea: "Longior et radius spatium descendere tantum / Certavit fessumque iubar vix inpulit imis" ("Its lengthened rays struggled to descend to such a depth and its weary glow reached the seabed only with difficulty"—5.600–601).

The Egyptian pursuit of the Jews into the sea evokes the next set of two speeches. The Pharaoh, still deluded, imagines that the moment of victory has come and drives his forces forward (5.605–608). The Egyptian army rushes to the sea and discovers the miraculously parted waters. One of their number, recognizing the reversal of natural law for what it is, a demonstration of supernatural intervention, delivers a speech of warning (5.620–35). He is, however, disregarded, and, as the Jews depart from the gulf, the Egyptians plunge into it.

In the final scene, Avitus accomplishes an impressive synthesis of themes. The Divinity, speaking through the pillar of fire, delivers the penultimate speech, directing Moses to use his rod to close the sea once again (5.653–58). In the following description, which recalls the watery spectacle of the preceding poem, the waters crash down on the Egyptians, and the Pharaoh, at the point of death, confesses his defeat, realizing too late that a human struggle was never to be: "Non haec humanis cedit victoria bellis; / Expugnamur, ait, caeloque evertimur hoste" ("This victory does not yield to human struggle. We are routed and overcome by a heavenly enemy"—5.672–73). Avitus then underlines the remorse-too-late theme and ends his narrative with a wonderfully executed tableau of the drowning army and its king. The details are vivid and carried by a verse that is rich in sound effects:

> Ergo exaltatis pendens sustollitur undis
> Mox mergenda phalanx: lympharum monte levata
> Pondere telorum premitur, fundoque tenaci
> Indutum revehunt morientia corpora ferrum.

(And so the enemy phalanx, on the very point of drowning, was lifted up and hung suspended on the rising waves. Because of the weight of their weapons, however, they sank into the rising

mountain of water and their dying bodies bore their iron
clothing to the sticky bottom.)                    (5.683–86)

This scene and Avitus' descriptions of the desperate Egyptian swim-
mers and the shipwreck of the Pharaoh's chariot not only are visually
compelling; they also recapitulate the central themes of the poem: the
reversal of natural and human events and the irony inherent in the illu-
sion of human competence, political, military or rhetorical, when not
informed by divine will.

Avitus ends his collection of biblical poems with a dazzling coda
(5.704–21) in which he moves in a few lines from Moses' hymn of tri-
umph, to the baptism of redeemed Christians, to the Fall of Adam and
Eve, to his own earlier poems, to the Redemption, prefigured in much
of his narrative and finally, with formulaic modesty, to a contrast be-
tween his five poems and the Pentateuch. This complex passage, in refer-
ring to the Redemption, looks back to the opening lines of his first
poem and closes the collection in upon itself in a ring structure. It also
reaffirms the poet's belief in the orthodox hermeneutic according to
which history is seen as a concatenation of figures signifying the
Redemption and Last Judgement.

# Prologue 2

The conclusion of the fifth poem leaves no doubt that Avitus saw it and
the four poems that precede it as a unit. This, as well as the fact that a
second prologue is affixed to the sixth poem, demonstrates that it was
written separately, published at a later date and intended to stand by it-
self. The sixth poem is not, however, entirely unrelated to Avitus'
earlier poetry. Quite the contrary, it complements the first five poems
in the collection. The earlier poems present the major events in human
history prior to the redemption of mankind; the sixth poem presents, in
a very different manner, the condition of humanity after its redemption.
The difference this historical complementarity implies is important for
understanding the final poem.

The sixth poem *is* very different. It is not a narrative but a didactic
and meditative work within which illustrative narratives are embedded.
In other words, the form of the earlier poems, narrative punctuated by
commentary, has been reversed. That reversal follows from the content
of the poem itself and the period of human history with which the poet

is now dealing. In his view there will be no historically significant events between the Redemption and the Last Judgement, which is seen by him as imminent. Avitus is, therefore living and writing in what he himself views as an essentially different period. There will be no cataclysmic events, supernaturally produced, as in the ages he dealt with in his earlier narratives. He lives in a world in which all are potentially elect, in which individual moral action is the only matter of importance. Not surprisingly, therefore, his final poem focuses upon the moral struggle of an individual. An analysis of his vision of that struggle, of the earthly conditions in which it must be conducted and finally of his role as a cleric and poet reveals much of interest about his age and the mentality of his contemporaries.

In addition to providing information about the publication of the sixth poem, Avitus' second prologue, which is also addressed to his brother, Apollinaris, provides two further indications of the poet's thoughts and intentions. First, to his reticence to publish and his formulaic self-denigration is added what appears to be a final renunciation of the writing of poetry, which he now views as an occupation inappropriate to both his years and his vocation. Avitus seems to have experienced even graver doubts about the use of rhetorical and poetic techniques drawn from Greece and Rome in the pursuit of his catachetical mission. He says:

> Decet enim dudum professionem, nunc etiam aetatem
> nostram, si quid scriptitandum est, graviori
> potius stilo operam ac tempus insumere
> nec in eo immorari, quod paucis intelligentibus
> mensuram syllabarum servando canat, sed quod
> legentibus multis mensurata fidei adstructione
> deserviat.

(Indeed for some time our calling and, more recently, our years have suggested that it is proper for us, if we must take pen in hand, to spend our time and effort on more serious literary themes, not squandering further days on a work that charms a few knowledgeable people by preserving a metrical pattern, but composing instead one which serves many readers with its measured instruction in the faith.)          (Prol. 2.2.9–12)

Ambivalence about the writing of poetry now verges on outright rejection. Not only is poetry not a privileged hermeneutic tool, its use by one dedicated to the saving of souls is scarcely proper. It is not surprising, in view of this, that in this final poem the didactic portions are central and a homiletic tone pervades the entire work.[40]

Second, the prologue also provides a clue to Avitus' immediate reason for composing yet one more poem in spite of his misgivings about versifying. He says to his brother: "Sane a faciendis versibus pedibusque iungendis pedem de cetero relaturus, nisi forte evidentis causae ratio extorserit alicuius epigrammatis necessitatem" ("You realize that I was on the point of abandoning the composition of poetry or verse on any new subject and would have done so, had not a clear and compelling reason turned me away from this resolve and toward the need for a short poem of this sort"—Prol. 2.2.6–8). What was the rare and compelling reason for the composition of the sixth poem? Clearly his sister, the nun Fuscina, was that reason, and the nature of the poem, which offers Fuscina consolation for her present self-denial and the promise of future praise and rewards in return for it, suggests that she may have been experiencing doubts about her vow of chastity. Finally, the fact that Avitus wrote a poem instead of a letter or even a sermon, which, one imagines, he might have arranged to deliver at Fuscina's convent, suggests that he considered his sister one of that group of educated contemporaries who were especially susceptible to the charms of verse. Both content and form, then, raise questions about the poet's view of women and sexuality. To explore this view further, we must turn to the poem itself.

## Poem 6

Avitus' meditation upon chastity falls into two parts. The first treats the relationship of faith to chastity and the liberating force of both. It is couched in biographical terms and is focused upon Fuscina and her family. The second deals with the translation or extension of faith and chastity into human action in the form of good works and consists largely of a series of *exempla* from scripture that act as behavioral prescriptions.

The poet begins by drawing a sharp contrast, consistent with his reflections in the prologue, between his poem, which will complement his

---

[40] Compare Prudentius' statement of the role of the Christian poet: *Carmina*, Prooemium 35–45 (*P.L.* 59.773–76), as well as that of the earlier poet, Juvencus, in his preface to the *Evangelicae Historiae*, Praefatio 23–35 (*P.L.* 19.59–62).

sister's liturgical observances, and the fraudulent inspiration and false poetry of Greece and Rome.[41] Tales such as that about Pegasus as well as the inspiration of the Muses and Apollo are tainted, he suggests, with "fallaci unda" ("waters of falsehood"—6.11), unlike his own poetry of which he says: "Dat tibi germanum sed verax musica plectrum / Et Christum resonans claudetur fistula Phoebo" ("truthful music presents you with a brother's plectrum true, and this, our pipe, echoing Christ, will be immune to Phoebus' inspiration"—6.17–18).

As he takes up their common family history, Avitus is, in fact, undertaking an examination of the calculus of grace that determines the eternal destiny of the redeemed man or woman. We are, in a sense, back in pre-lapsarian Eden, with two important differences: Satan's temptation can now be effective for individuals only and grace, a countervailing force, is now available to humanity. The interaction of these two powers in his own world will be Avitus' central concern in this poem, and it will soon become clear that, whereas in the Edenic poems God's blessings were largely physical and Satan's temptation largely intellectual, in the poet's own age temptation is largely physical and sexual, and grace is intellectual. In short, an understanding of Christ's redemptive act will, in this orthodox reckoning, lead to liberation from physicality. We are presented with a Platonic ethical scheme and an idealized moral symmetry. At the same time, Avitus' keen observation of human behavior, functioning as an elaborative tool in the shaping of his discourse, also reveals some of the harsh reality that lay beneath the theological and moral struggle he depicts.

One is immediately struck, for example, by the prominence of sickness and death in his picture of contemporary life. Ornamental jewelry is referred to as: "Ornatusque ... qui membra venustant, / Quae mox pascendis praebebunt vermibus escas, / Et forsan dum vita manet" ("ornaments that grace limbs soon to provide food for worms, perhaps even while life remains in them"—6.45–47). In fact Avitus displays a physician's interest in the nature of physical decline and death and proposes a theory of morbidity according to which the human body suffers from a kind of contest of diseases in which one disease eventually gains the upper hand and kills as the others withdraw: "Omnia dum proprio solvantur corpora fine / Atque unus praestet reliquos desistere casus" ("All bodies find their own dissolution as one sickness carries the day

---

[41] See note 5, page 4.

and all others retreat"—6.51-52). In other words, life is for him little
more than a battlefield on which various forms of death contend.

This pervasive threat of sickness and death appears to have burdened
women in special ways. Avitus' own mother, Audentia, after bearing
many children, not only took a vow of chastity herself but also took a
vow of virginity on behalf of Fuscina, her last child. These decisions
suggest her own desperation as well as a desire to spare her daughter the
perilous experience of giving birth to many children.

Avitus underlines the fact that the agonies which death and illness
brought to women's lives are frequently produced by sexuality itself,
agonies that echo the judgement of Eve in the third poem. Procreation
and sexuality evoke from Avitus a litany of the horrors and catastrophes
that attend wedded life and childbirth.[42] A married woman is:
"subiecta viro" ("subject to a man"—6.168) and "Servit in obsceno ...
lecto" ("serves in a disgusting bed"—6.169). Sexuality itself breeds death
in many ways (6.181-97). Avitus reminds his sister that mothers die in
childbirth, leaving orphans behind, children die with their mothers, chil-
dren die alone at birth and, unbaptized, are plunged into Hell. And even
if childbirth goes well, he adds, children often die in their youth, cheat-
ing mothers of their hope and joy.

This grim vision is, of course, rhetorical and, in all likelihood, in-
tended to persuade a sister having doubts about her vocation, but it
must reflect to some extent the situation of women in Avitus' age. Fam-
ilies were large and many females were produced. Fuscina was, we are
told, her mother's fourth daughter. For many well-born women there
may have been few options outside the convent wall. As we have seen,
Fuscina herself was dedicated to the religious life at birth and took her
vows as a child of ten. In encouraging her, Avitus presents a long list of
family women who, early in their lives or late, entered the convent
(6.81-108). Among their role models we find Machabaea who had so lit-
tle regard for procreation that she rejoiced at the death of her child:
"prolis funere felix, / Orbari gaudens animo vincente senectam" ("she
rejoiced in the death of a child, with a mind victorious, rejoiced that her
old age was deprived"—6.105-106).

This prescription of the intellectual mastery of a debased sexuality
follows from the idea that the grasping of salvation is first an intellectual

---

[42] A shorter but similar list of the trials attending marriage and childbearing is found in
Jerome, *Epistola XXII ad Eustochium* 2 (*P.L.* 22:395).

act, an act that will imitate but transcend physical procreativity. Thus Avitus says to Fuscina: "Tu germana, pium quem ducis ab ubere fascem, / Non carnis, sed legis habes cervice fideli / Subdita ferre iugum nec vincla in coniugis ire" ("You, my sister, hold on your devoted shoulder the holy burden, which you bring forth from your mother's breast, not according to the flesh, but the law, you who are bent to bear a yoke but not to accept the bonds of marriage"—6.154–56). Physical procreativity is to be transformed into intellectual or spiritual procreativity, which continues to be described in physical terms.[43] Thus Christ is said to have received the infant Fuscina "in cunis" ("in her cradle"—6.26), and she is told: "Scriberis in thalamos ac magni foedera regis / Et cupit electam speciem sibi iungere Christus" ("You are enrolled as a consort, are wedded to a mighty king, and Christ wants to join Himself to your beautiful form which He has selected"—6.65–66). It becomes clear as Avitus continues that Christ's redemptive act has also redeemed fallen human sexuality by permitting it to rise above mere physicality. For women, the central figure signifying this transformation is, of course, the Virgin. Avitus reminds his sister: "Tu Mariam sequeris, dono cui contigit alto / Virginis et matris gemina gaudere corona, / Conciperet cum carne deum" ("You follow Mary who was permitted under Heaven's dispensation to rejoice in the twin crown, that of both virgin and mother, when she conceived God in the flesh"—6.201–203). Fuscina imitates the Virgin by bearing Christ intellectually, and this is essentially a liberating act.[44] After enumerating the horrors that attend physical sexuality, Avitus insists that his sister is free of all of these: "At late longeque tuam discernere sortem / Libertas cum lege potest, qua necteris, ut te / Impia fallentis non stringant vincla mundi" ("But under the rule by which you are now bound a new freedom has the power to move your life to a place distant and remote from these things, and as a result the unholy bonds of the false world do not hold you fast" (6.198–200). The end result of this liberation is the creation of a realm, analogous to Paradise, in which physical sexuality is irrelevant.[45]

---

[43] For a discussion of the erotic dimension in women's devotions in the Middle Ages, see E. A. Petroff, *Medieval Women's Visionary Literature* (Oxford: Oxford Univ. Press, 1986), 5–20. See also Jerome, *Epistola XXII ad Eustochium* 25 (*P.L.* 22:411).

[44] The liberation offered is, of course, based upon devotion to a male Divinity in a manner prescribed by a male hierarchy. A religious woman's autonomy was, therefore, severely circumscribed and constrained.

[45] See note 19, page 30.

To emphasize this, Avitus closes the first half of the sixth poem (6.223–81) with an account of the special privilege given to the women at the tomb of the Redeemer (Mt. 28.1–10), an account that gives him the opportunity to present another spectacular angelic appearance and to include Christ's dramatic encounter with the women as they make their way from the tomb. Avitus closes this passage with the following reaffirmation by the disciples that gender is irrelevant to salvation: "Agnoscunt animum potius quam vincere sexum" ("They recognized that mind and not gender carried off the palm of victory"—6.281).

Faith may produce a realm in which sex and gender are irrelevant, but Avitus insists that the temptations of the flesh continue to threaten, and, if we may judge from his text, that women, whose special weakness has already been emphasized in the second poem,[46] are especially vulnerable. Even in the biblical scene described above the angel instructs the women at the tomb: "Femineo sexu mentes transite viriles" ("In your woman's sex excel even a man's mind"—6.257). It is this special weakness and the remedies for it that will concern Avitus in the second half of this poem. How, he asks, can the individual, in this case his sister, having made an act of faith and taken a vow of chastity, keep from slipping back into bondage to sensuality?

The answer to this question springs from the poet's understanding of his age. Avitus' view of the period of history which follows the Redemption and precedes the Last Judgement assumes that all aspects of life, physical and spiritual, are extremely precarious.[47] We have already seen evidence of this view in his description of the material circumstances of post-lapsarian life in the third poem, and Avitus further elaborates his estimate of his own perilous age, emphasizing spiritual danger, in this poem:

> Nil non incertum praesentia saecula ducunt
> Nec secura datur requies in carne caduca.
> Vertuntur nam saepe boni, perit obruta virtus
> Partaque transactae decedunt praemia laudis.

---

[46] For Prudentius women are *male fortis* or feebler and have a *mens fragilis*, a frail intelligence, *Hamartigenia* 277–78 (*P.L.* 59:1031). In similar fashion Dracontius, *Carmen de Deo* 1:468–69 (*P.L.* 60:730), contrasts Adam's *fortia corda* with Eve, who is *pietatis inops*.

[47] This vision of human existence resembles that presented by Boethius in the *De consolatione philosophiae*, in which Fortuna is seen as the cause of the instability in human affairs. In his fourth book, however, Boethius concludes that all fortune, however fickle, is in the end guided by providence and hence good (4.7 [*P.L.* 63:823–25]).

(For this present existence offers nothing certain and no rest from care is granted to those who wear this dying flesh. Often the good are brought low, virtue is vanquished and perishes and the rewards of glory achieved in the past recede from view.)

(6.122–25)

Spiritual jeopardy results above all from *otium* or indolence, and for this reason Avitus stresses the importance of good works:

> Nam studium sancti laxet si forte laboris
> Pigraque consuetas dissolvant otia curas,
> Labitur in praeceps damnosae gloria vitae.

(For if it happens that zeal in holy works is relaxed and if lazy indolence undoes our customary prudence, then the glory of life, doomed in the end, falls headlong away.)          (6.132–34)

This counsel against *otium* and prescription of *studium sancti laboris* is three times reinforced by biblical *exempla*.[48] The first (6.290–337) is the story of the three servants tested with a gift of money, which their master, represented here as God Himself, instructs them to invest wisely in His absence (Mt. 25.14–30 and Lk. 19.12–27). It is introduced with a clear warning about the necessity of work: "adtento desudet vita labore" ("life must sweat and never rest from struggle"—6.285), and goes on to describe the use each of the servants made of the money given to him. The course followed by the two wise servants is instructive: one gives his money to the poor; the second uses it to spread the gospel. In both cases, the money, metaphorically transformed, reaps a great profit, suggesting that almsgiving and catachetical instruction are prominent among the good works which Avitus is prescribing.

The next two parables are presented together. The first (6.417–24) is the tale of Christ's curse on the barren fig tree (Mt. 21.18–19 and Mk. 11.12–14, 20–25), the second (6.445–91) the story of the foolish virgins, who were, according to the story in the gospel (Mt. 25.1–13), unprepared for the arrival of the bridegroom. The parable of the fig tree is ad-

---

[48] I have organized the seven *exempla* given by Avitus in the second half of this poem into two groups: those which are counsels against *otium* (6.290–387, 6.417–24, and 6.445–91) and those which appear to be examples of strategies for overcoming it (6.342–62, 6.503–27, 6.534–48, and 6.549–620). They are in fact intertwined in the text.

monitory only and contains no hint of the nature of the work the pious Christian must perform. It makes most explicit, however, the insufficiency of virginity alone: "Sic et virginitas sacro devota pudori / Indiget adiunctis virtutibus" ("And so virginity, which is dedicated to holy modesty, needs other virtues to accompany it"—6.430-31). What are these virtues? In what works are they realized? The parable of the foolish virgins, which follows this passage, takes us little further in understanding Avitus' counsel. Presumably the bridegroom signifies Christ, and the wise virgins are the types of chaste women like Fuscina who become His brides or handmaidens. And what, then, are their good works? We can in fact find very little beyond the fact that they were vigilant, that they persevered and made the proper preparations.

Does Avitus ever go beyond this prescription of almsgiving, preaching, and vigilance in his treatment of good works? We have already seen, earlier in the poem, a reference to the chanting of psalms and the reading of edifying works. This counsel is, in fact, carried further. Avitus presents his sister with a long reading list which includes not only the books of the Old and New Testaments but also: "quid sacrum nostri cecinere poetae" ("anything holy our poets write"—6.409). In short, he is constructing a canon of works, whose reading may be classed as *sanctus labor*. His inclusion of Christian poetry, if only that which contains what is *sanctum* and is written by *nostri poetae*, is reassuring, given his own rejection of poetic authority in the prologue.[49] Furthermore, his remarks about his sister's sophistication as a reader, about her ability to receive Latin verse, cannot but confirm our earlier hypothesis that he considered Fuscina an especially apt candidate for instruction through poetry.[50] Avitus seems, however, to remain ambivalent about this. He admires her skill and ability: "agnoscis leges et commata servas / Atque aliena tuo commendas carmina cantu" ("You understand syntax and metrics and so can add grace to another's verse as you read"—6.410-11). But he also feels compelled to add: "Et quae nota tibi vel quae percursa legendo, / Ad virtutis opus studio converte virili" ("with a manly zeal

---

[49] On reading habits in the fifth century, see Sidonius Apollinaris, *Epistolae* 2:9 (*P.L.* 58:483-86). In the same collection, 2:10 (*P.L.* 58:486-88) and 4:17 (*P.L.* 58:521-22) he remarks upon the decline of the quality of writing in Latin.

[50] Unlike women in later ages, who, according to Walter Ong S.J., were not admitted to academia where Latin was learned, *Orality and Literature* (New York: Methuen, 1982), 113-14, Fuscina had learned to read difficult Latin texts with discernment.

turn what you know or what you have merely skimmed in your reading
into a work of virtue"—6.413-14). In other words, reading is morally am-
biguous. If pursued in a feminine way, it runs the risk of being nothing
more than a distraction and therefore of failing to qualify as a *sanctus labor*.

Avitus presents to his sister four additional *exempla*, three from scrip-
ture, one from his own era, and these ought to provide some indication
of the kind of reading he is advocating. It will be useful to examine these
four stories both to test the validity of his fears about the attitudes of
the female reader and to search in them for further examples of good
works beyond those, including study, which we have found in his text.
The story that introduces Avitus' advocacy of devotional reading (6.342-
62) is the biblical tale of Deborah, the prophetess responsible for the de-
feat of the Canaanite general Sisarra and for his subsequent death at the
hands of another woman (Judges 4). It is a violent and bloody anecdote
which Avitus tidies up by transforming Deborah's bloodthirsty valor in-
to the spiritual resources of virginity and its powers to overcome
"foeda libido" ("foul desire"—6.374) and its phallic ally, the first poem's
"aemulus anguis" ("jealous snake"—6.376). This transformation of the
episode into a sexual encounter foreshadows the focus of the three fol-
lowing *exempla*, all of which have a sexual theme.

Significantly, the next tale (6.503-27), drawn not from scripture but
from history, is about the transvestite saint, Eugenia, who, after being
made an abbot, was falsely accused of making sexual advances by a
young woman, who, believing her a man, became infatuated with her.
Eugenia extricated herself from this situation by at last revealing that she
was a woman, thus preserving both her virginity and her unstained rep-
utation. The story is told in some detail and is followed (6.534-48) by a
treatment of the biblical tale of Joseph and Potiphar's wife (Gn. 39-41).
The final *exemplum* (6.549-620) is the biblical story (Apocrypha: Daniel
and Susanna) of the attempted seduction of Susanna by two older men
and of her rescue by Daniel, whose biography, including lions and an
airborne lunch, is included in Avitus' version.[51]

These three stories are revealing. They resemble, in fact, a modern
genre, the romantic short story. The first and third also bring to mind
the kind of confessional fiction that has often been directed at a stereo-

---

[51] See note 29, page 40. The prophet who brings Daniel food is Habakuk. The scene is
pictured in the central ceiling panel of the Lateran Palace's Daniel room in Rome.

typical female imagination. Avitus' misgivings become, then, more understandable. His own age of dramatic reversals of all sorts no doubt evoked an interest in this kind of romantic tale, and his sister's nature and education appears to have rendered her susceptible to the charms of the genre, especially when rendered in verse. In short, Avitus was faced with a dilemma. He wanted to grasp Fuscina's imagination forcefully, but he also wanted her to read with a "studio virili" ("manly zeal") and to conclude that she should persevere in her chaste life. He did what he had to do: he told the stories and drew from them a suitably orthodox lesson. As he notes before introducing the story of Eugenia: "Fragiles nam carne puellas / Protulit interdum caelo constantia mentis" ("For an unswerving resolve has sometimes raised even maidens whose flesh is weak to Heaven"—6.501-502). This was, one assumes, the result he hoped for in presenting his sister with these romantic narratives.

The story of Eugenia is, of course, especially interesting because its heroine assumes not only the mental and spiritual attributes of a man, as Avitus is recommending, but, at least in her office and dress, the physical and political attributes as well. Why did Avitus include this paradigmatic tale? It is not unlikely that he did so to make sure that his sister would understand the limitations placed upon the assumption of masculine attitudes and roles. Fuscina may display the intellectual and spiritual strength of a man, but she may not, as the tale of Eugenia demonstrates, *become* a man or take on the powers and prerogatives of a man within the ecclesiastical hierarchy.

One of the above stories deals with a woman who sinned and confessed, one with a man sinned against and justified and one with a woman who engaged in gender-deception. Can we find in these *exempla* any further indication of what kinds of *sanctus labor* Avitus is recommending for his sister? Not much. Patience, perseverance and fortitude in the face of temptation are clearly the qualities recommended, but if we search for other concrete activities with which to banish *otium*, we search in vain. Indeed Avitus seems to underline this conclusion in the penultimate stanza of the poem (6.621-45). His final argument looks to the reward for virginity at the Last Judgement. That reward will be, he tells his sister, greater than the reward given to faithful wives.[52] To

---

[52] Methodius says that virgins will be the first in the procession behind Christ in Paradise, *Symposium* 7:3 (*P.G.* 18:127-30). Tertullian, following Paul, 1 Cor. 7.9, affirms that chastity is superior to marriage, *Ad uxorem* 1:3 (*P.L.* 1:1277-79), and places virgins closer to God, 1:8 (*P.L.* 1:1287-88).

emphasize this, he tells the story of Martha, who complained to Christ about the fact that her sister was listening to Him and not assisting with the preparation of their meal (Lk. 10.38-42). To this Christ replied: "Sunt plurima quae te / Obstrictam retinent, melior sed causa quietae / Lectaque nec poterit Mariae pars optima tolli" ("There are many things which can hold you fast, but the better thing has been chosen by Mary who is not caught up in the world's work, and this, which is the best portion, cannot be taken from her"—6.643-45).[53]

And so it appears that, as salvation is seen as intellectually grasped, the cures for *otium* are also intellectual. Only almsgiving stands with them in Avitus' text as a second example of *sanctus labor*. Or perhaps not quite. Avitus' closing stanza (6.646-66) suggests to Fuscina that she herself must work to become an *exemplum*.[54] This stanza touches once again on their common family tradition, contrasting the worldly and spiritual achievements of that family's members, clearly giving precedence to their spiritual works. Its moral lesson follows naturally from the signifying moment to which this passage looks, the consummation of human history, the Second Coming and the Last Judgement. In its light, the human actors in the providential plan of the Creator participate in the creation of a text in which they are themselves signifiers, *exempla, figurae*. Human action constitutes a kind of evolving hagiographical tradition in which, as in Dante later, the position of each saint is determined by his or her intellectual or spiritual message, not by earthly status or achievement. In this framework, Avitus correctly closes this poem to his sister with the following bold conceit: "materque effecta parentum / Virgineae victrix sociabere laeta catervae" ("having become the spiritual mother of your own forebears, you are joined in victory and joy with their virgin company"—6.665-66).

The scriptural paraphrase in this final poem is, as we have noted, different from that in the earlier poems, for here the passages drawn from the Bible are embedded in an essentially meditative and discursive text. There is, however, another more striking difference. In this poem the nature of the paraphrases illustrates the central proposition of the text itself. If salvation in the age of Avitus and his sister is largely dependent upon an intellectual response to grace, then meditation, reading and in-

---

[53] On this passage from scripture and the transitory nature of daily human work, see Augustine, *Sermones* 255 (*P.L.* 39:1186).

[54] Petroff, *Medieval Women's Visionary Literature*, 64-5, discusses the role of women as spiritual leaders and *exempla*, with special reference to Saints Thecla and Macrina.

terpretation are central to the Christian moral struggle. The sixth poem may be read, therefore, as a proposed curriculum that presents both a reading list and, more important, a theoretical model for the interpretation of texts. The model is formulated in part on the basis of gender, for Fuscina is instructed to turn random, one is tempted to suggest "feminine," reading into a *"sanctus labor"* by approaching the texts as Avitus himself would.

The paraphrases here must, therefore, be read on two levels, for their content as well as for their form and for the interpretative strategies that form suggests. As we have noted, Fuscina possessed the linguistic and grammatical skills required for the reception of the recommended texts. What Avitus supplies are the hermeneutic skills. Fuscina must learn first to select, as Avitus has, the readings that meet her spiritual needs, then she must learn to interpret them in accordance with the orthodox discursive authority which he himself represented.

We must conclude, therefore that Avitus' paraphrases in this poem mirror the concerns found in his prologues. In the prologues he revealed his fears about license in producing texts; here he reveals a similar fear about license in their reception. What we find in both cases is an anxiety about the polysemous power of poetic texts on the part of an individual who sees salvation as depending in part on precisely the opposite linguistic phenomenon: the rigid control of signification in texts in accordance with orthodox sensibility. It is his fear that Fuscina will bring to texts a different, feminine sensibility, that has at least in part driven him to produce this final poem. As we have noted, he is fighting fire with fire, providing in poetry properly conceived and received an antidote to the seductiveness of misused texts.[55]

## *Conclusion*

A consideration of Avitus' poems confirms and expands the hypotheses presented at the beginning of this introduction to his work. First, his treatment of human sexuality casts light upon the complex dia-

---

[55] In considering the levels on which this poem moves, one cannot help but wonder whether Avitus did not have Revelations in mind when he brought his family's triumphant procession to a close on line 666. A poet who played upon number at the conclusion of the *S.H.G.* may well have enjoyed this symbolic treading on the ancient adversary at the end of his final poem.

lectical relationship between the orthodox view of women and their pro-
creative role and the actual conditions, physical and psychological, they
experienced in the poet's own age. In his pre-lapsarian world, sexuality
and indeed physicality are seen as good, although some weakness seems
to inhere in female sexuality, while intellect, at least when freed of di-
vine rule, is evil. In Avitus' own world, this relationship is reversed.
Sensuality and sexuality are seen as obstacles to the achieving of salva-
tion, the path to which is intellectual and spiritual. The status of women
in Avitus' age is, therefore, ambiguous. Although clearly redeemed and
potentially among God's elect, they represent in a special way the dis-
tractions of the physical world. As we have seen, their lives, as described
by Avitus, were beset not only by the psychological contradictions in-
herent in this orthodox view but by considerable insecurity, and fear.
For those who shared Avitus' view of history and the economy of grace,
sexual interaction must have been perceived as diminishing human love
of the Divinity and, with the Second Coming not far off,[56] physical
procreation had very little compensatory value, as Avitus himself makes
clear. In short, many women in fifth- and sixth-century Gaul appear to
have found themselves in a social and intellectual paradigm in which
neither human affection in sex nor the raising of children played a sig-
nificant role in the economy of grace and salvation. This dilemma must
have further aggravated their already precarious lives.

Another of our initial hypotheses suggested that a central vision of
human history informs Avitus' poetry and determines his own herme-
neutical approach to the content of his text, an approach sometimes at
odds with some of his own instincts and with other intellectual tradi-
tions with which he had to work. His poems have indeed proved to be
both elaborations of the orthodox Christian world view and studies in
the tension between it and other interpretative approaches. At every
level, historical, theological, moral and eschatological, Avitus' literary
techniques depend upon and are nourished by his vision of the historical
plenum which stretches from Creation to the *eschaton*, in which the sig-
nificance of every act is understood only in terms of the totality and es-
pecially of the end. This historical *totum simul* is the source of all signi-
fication. This is, in other words, a world in which everything is a *figura*

---

[56] The *tempus est breve* theme is common in this age. See, for example, Tertullian, *De ex-
hortatione castitatis* 6 (*P.L.* 2:921) and *Ad uxorem* 1:5 (*P.L.* 1282–83).

and in which metaphor and reality are one.[57] As we have seen, this orthodox Christian view presented Avitus the poet with difficulties at three levels. First, it was not congruent with the orthodox Jewish inter-pretation of the scriptural matter with which he had to deal.[58] Second, it clashed with both the literary and philosophical traditions of Greece and Rome in which he was educated and whose literary genres he was employing. And finally, it constrained his own curiosity and interest in the empirical observation of natural and human phenomena. Seen from this perspective, Avitus' poems are studies in intellectual and literary accommodation and revision. They enable us to see with remarkable clarity the manner in which intellectual paradigms and their her-meneutical strategies were rejected because they appeared to be irrecon-cilable with the closed and seemingly perfect system of signification which intellectual authority espoused. There is some evidence in Avitus' poems that suggests that his age, still in possession of Greek and Roman thought about nature and mankind, might yet have achieved further in-tellectual progress in these areas, employing that thought as a starting point. There is also much in his poetry to demonstrate why this kind of advance was becoming increasingly unlikely.[59]

One further conclusion, related to this second one, has, it seems to me, emerged, particularly in light of the contents of the sixth poem. If Avitus' intellectual world is circumscribed and limited by the orthodox view of human history, his view of human action in history is no less constrained and limited. For him, man after the Redemption lives in a curious gray age in which the final transactions under the economy of divine grace work themselves out. The script or scenario of that age is a given and is, in human terms at least, seemingly irrational. The events in the scenario are dramatic in the theatrical sense; they provide a plot through which the *ethos* of the individual actors emerges, i.e., their

---

[57] See Eric Auerbach on the relation of *littera figura* and *veritas* in this scheme: "Figura" in *Scenes from the Drama of European Literature* (New York: Meridian, 1959), 11–76.

[58] Avitus' assimilation of Jewish history in these poems is a good example of Christi-anity's determination to recast Jewish tradition.

[59] The attitudes of early Christian thinkers to ancient philosophy vary widely, of course. Among the most positive is that of Boethius, who revered philosophy and saw it as an in-dispensable human tool. Even Sidonius Apollinaris tells a bishop that he has been wed to philosophy (albeit suitably purged of error), *Epistola* 9:9 (*P.L.* 58:622–28). Augustine's judgement is more measured. He recognizes some of the insights of Platonism but finds philosophical moralizing generally ineffective, *Civitas Dei* 8:5–13 and 2:7 (*P.L.* 41:229–38). Avitus must be placed among the most negative of the poets, although Prudentius' view is also basically negative, *Apotheosis* 200–11 (*P.L.* 59:938–40).

moral status and salvation are determined. In Avitus, the notion that the scenario itself can be rewritten or revised by man is virtually absent. If human beings act as secondary causes, it is merely to assist one another, often as *exempla*, as Avitus advises his sister, in reacting properly to the vagaries of the historical plot and the spiritual dangers it presents. Not only has the intellectual curiosity of the Greek thinkers fallen under a cloud, but also, it seems, the Roman hope for establishing an orderly realm in which human pain is curtailed and a civilized and tranquil commonwealth secured. In short, we see in his poetry a rapid fading of faith in the city of man and an increasing reliance upon and faith in the city of God.[60]

Unquestionably, Avitus is, in all of this, particularly conservative and rigid for his own age. Other thinkers and poets take what seems to us a more enlightened approach to both intellectual discourse and social and political action. We should recall, however, that Avitus, as a prominent churchman, represents the establishment in a special way. It was inevitable that his view would grow in privilege as the social and ecclesiastical system of the medieval world developed. To that extent he is, it seems to me, a significant harbinger of the intellectual and social world of the following centuries, in which literary and theological prescriptions similar to his would increasingly influence both the canon of medieval literary works and the focus of human action.[61]

---

[60] Augustine rejects the idea that we can rely upon friends and the efforts of good men, *Civitas Dei* 19:8 (*P.L.* 41:634–35), and insists that human miseries are removed only through grace, 22:22 (*P.L.* 41:784–87).

[61] It is interesting to note, in conclusion, that the social and intellectual paradigms that Avitus' reading of Christian revelation produced are revised in the last great Christian epic, Milton's *Paradise Lost*. This revision is the subject of M. Grossman's *Authors to Themselves* (Cambridge: Cambridge Univ. Press, 1987), in which he argues that changes in economic and social patterns in the sixteenth and seventeenth centuries produced a new Christian concept of self that redefines the individual as an effective secondary cause, relocates divine order in history, and introduces the notion of human progress.

# Translation

## *Prologue 1*

To my holy Lord in Christ, Apollinaris, Bishop, most pious and blessed, his brother, Alcimus Ecdicius Avitus, sends greetings.

Not long ago, after gathering a few of my sermons into a single collection, I did in fact decide, with the encouragement of my friends, to publish them. But now, since you urge an even more substantial undertaking, I have steeled myself and am turning to a literary endeavor of greater boldness and daring. And indeed you enjoin me, if I have written poetry on any subject whatever, to set a dedication to you beneath the work's title page. I did in fact recall that I had written a number of verses, so many in fact that, had they been brought together in a collection, the number of the poems would have filled a sizable volume. But while I was giving thought to this undertaking, taking care to keep the material in the proper sequence according both to subject and date, almost all of it was scattered and lost in the difficulties which our recent and widely known disorders occasioned. Since it would be difficult to search for each and every one of these and impossible to find them, I put from my mind those works whose reorganization, in the case of those still in my possession, and whose restoration, in the case of those that had disappeared, seemed to me so hard. Later, I did indeed come upon some notebooks that a friend of mine had. These works, although they generally hold to the subjects their titles suggest, touch upon other matters as well whenever the material provides an opportunity. It is these then which, although undistinguished in workmanship, are to be embellished by your name, since it is you who ask for their publication. You realize, I am sure, that a man may be as clever and learned as you like, but if he maintains a style that befits his religious convictions, observing the laws of faith no less than those of metrics, he is little suited to the composition of poetry. Indeed, although a kind of freedom to tell false tales is granted equally to painters and poets, this freedom must be utterly banished from serious subject matter. You know how it is with the composition of worldly verse: the more elegantly, rather I should say the more foolishly one decks out false tales, the more accomplished one is considered. I need not mention the words and terms which we ought not dote on in the works of others, let alone write in our own, which in the elliptical style of poets often signify one thing by another. And so, although worldly critics, who attribute my refusal to employ the license of poets to a lack of either skill or diligence, may judge that I have embarked upon a work more arduous than profitable, I nevertheless insist on making a broad and clear distinction between divine judgement and their own human criticism. And indeed I do believe that a cleric who is a poet, if he must err in some way in treating or, if need be, in explaining subject matter of any kind, works more good if he falls short in literary ostentation rather than in obedience to the rule of his life, is safer if he lets his verse limp, rather than fail to track the truth. Literary license is certainly not an excuse for the committing of sin. For if we assume that for every *idle* word men have spoken they must give a reckoning, if a poet gives preference to the laws of language rather than to the laws of life, it is clearly manifest that his word, which has been carefully considered and employed, is fraught with greater spiritual danger and harm.

## 1. The Beginning of the World

To you, Adam, our first father, I shall attribute the cause of mankind's various suffering, to you the reason why our mortal life possesses so brief a span. To you I shall attribute, moreover, the fact that our tainted nature is in its very origin infected, that nature which acts not ours but of our ancient parents still weigh down. Yes, although I recognize that our own guilt plays its part as well, the fact that our natural dignity has for all this time continued to be lost in sin I shall ascribe to you, who with the seed of death did pluck the living bud from the doomed race of your successors. And although Christ took all this, our debt, upon himself and discharged it, as much as our race in its stricken stock did owe, nevertheless, because of the sin of our author, who contracted the debt of mortality and sent sickness and death upon his descendants, the scar of his transgression lives in our death-ridden flesh.

Now the Almighty Father, creating equilibrium with the weight of His word alone, gathered the waters together from all sides and set apart the dry land, confining the sea within its shores and the rivers within their banks. Now with a beautiful light, as the day of darkness receded, He displayed the proper shapes of things, and His abundant grace decked with color the newly apportioned world. Then, with the coming of time, the lights received their turns to shine in the sky, as sun and moon made alternating journeys. And more than that, in the hours that belong to night, starlight softened the gloomy darkness with a sidereal glow. In a moment the lovely earth, its labor a delight, brought forth all kinds of growth and was clothed with sudden vegetation. What was ordered to be made received its being without the germ of procreation, and His mere willing of it was its seed. And so, by the fertility of His word, the forests put forth their leaves, and in an instant the tree, springing from tender roots, made its broad branches hard.

All at once animals of all kinds grew into their ugly shapes, and these brute creatures ran here and there through the empty world. Carried aloft and suspended by the rapid flapping of their feathers, birds cut their paths through the sky and in the bright air balanced the weight of their bodies on nimble wings. Next, the fish, enclosed beneath the vast ocean's flood, breathed in the water and drew breath beneath the surface of the sea. Indeed the moisture itself gave them life, which it denies to us. So too did great whales thrive in the sea and occupy a fitting dwelling place within its hollow recesses. The Creator's fashioning skill fitted to enormous shapes monsters the sea now rarely sends forth. And yet we should remember that what the ignorant mind of men mistakenly believes to be ugly, when seen for what it is, is beautiful in nature's judgement.

And so, when everything shone forth and all things were completed, when the world stood finished and perfect in its own adornment, in eternal light the Almighty Father turned His joyful countenance from the lofty vault of Heaven down to earth, brightening as He did whatever He looked upon, and His works pleased their architect as He gazed upon them, and the Creator praised the earth He had built, arranged as it was in its own beautiful order. Then at last Wisdom spoke, saying, "Behold how this bright fabric shines with earthly decoration. And yet, what further joy can there be when a world filled with every perfection has no possessor to tend it? No, to keep long inactivity from casting gloom over this new earth, now let man be formed, man whom the image of Our mighty Godhead will touch, and endowed with high honor, let him assume Our nature within his noble mind. It pleases Us to place this creature with countenance erect in charge of the four-footed beasts, he who, under an eternal covenant, will rule the subject earth, subdue the brute animals, give to all of them names and laws and note the stars and the paths of Heaven. Let him understand the heavenly bodies and learn to distinguish the seasons by watching their signs. Let him subdue the savage sea and with his tenacious ingenuity possess whatever he sees. Let the beast with gnashing teeth serve him and let bulls and horses be tamed, once their fury is put aside. Let them learn to endure his rule and let the frightened pack animals hasten at his command to be bound with fetters they know and accept. And so that Man's nature may stand out as even more sublime, let it be his special gift to carry a countenance that gazes up to Heaven. Let him seek out his own Maker to Whom he may, long-lived in years, devoutly render a life of servitude."

These things God spoke and, deigning to touch the brittle earth, He mingled wet mud with sprinkled dust. Then His profound Wisdom fashioned a new body. This is just the way an artist now creates, an artist who uses his skill to shape the soft wax that yields all kinds of shapes beneath his touch, as he molds a face with his hand, fashions a body of plaster or arranges features in a piece of clay. This is the way the Almighty Father went on molding the earth that was destined for life, as He designed the body from the soft mud. Then, at that body's lofty crest, He marked the head's tower, fitting a countenance with seven openings to the senses, which bring understanding and are capable of smelling, hearing, seeing and tasting. Touch would be the only one which, as arbiter, would feel sensations everywhere in the body and scatter its own special power through the limbs. A flexible tongue He enclosed within a hollow palate in such a way that, confined in that chamber, the strokes of the pulsing instrument would cause measured speech to sound in the air when it was struck. Next, the tapering breast on that straight body pushed forth fingered hands at the ends of strong arms. In the middle of the body, beneath the stomach, a place was allotted to the abdomen, which, with its soft cover, protects the vital organs that lie between the body's two sides. The thigh was divided so that it might more easily move both limbs one after the other and walk with flexed knees. On the other side of the body, which a single Creator formed, the neck began to slope from beneath its place under the head and to add great sinews to the body's joints. A rigid spine, with many knots at the connecting places, caused the double cage of ribs to branch out in order, and the inside of the body was formed for new vital functions, its life-sustaining organs providing at the same time a natural protection for the heart whose mass hung hidden beneath these closely fitted inner parts. Next, the lungs, destined to be fed by the insubstantial air, were added to draw in and accept the breath of gentle wind they would receive and then, exhaling, to give back what they inhaled. Now in, now out, their breathing would run on and on with these frequent inhalations. The right side of the body held the fountain of the liver, which the blood would invigorate and by which the veins would scatter their enclosed stream through the body. The spleen, the stabilizer of this system, received the left side and because of it, they say, the hair and nails we cut grow back again, those very nails, which as they do the body's work, enjoy life but no sensation. Nor do they feel pain when they are cut, for, once pared, they begin to grow longer again.

After the image of this perfect new creature lay finished and the molded clay had taken on all the appearances their Maker desired, the mud became flesh. What was soft grew hard, and the bones drew their marrow from within the body. Blood filled the veins, and a flush tinged the face with the color of life. Its original pallor was driven from the entire body, and the snowy face was painted red. Then, when the whole man grew used to being alive, with his limbs now finished, and as the body grew steamy with warmth, the soul alone was wanting, the soul which the Creator would produce from an untainted source and place as ruler in the upright frame. From His eternal lips He poured forth a gentle breath and breathed upon man, and man, when he had caught the breath, at once drew it in and learned how to breathe regularly.

After wisdom that looks ahead imbued his newborn senses and they glowed with the pure light of reason, he arose and, standing upright, placed his feet upon the earth. Then, as he marvelled at the dappled vision of the world and at the resplendent heaven, the Creator addressed him in these words: "All this profusion of beauty you behold among the earth's new furnishings, extending as they do throughout this decorated globe, hold as yours alone and, as the very first man, rule and enjoy them all. But here is My greatest command: as everything serves you, so do you serve Me and obey your devoted Father who subjects all this to you. Worship no other images or empty gods, nothing sublime and strange that may flash out in the sky, not the shapes that live on the earth or in the water, not that which nature, by her own restrictions, may keep from sight. These are, remember, for your use and not for adoration. As you surpass His creatures, bow down and adore your Creator."

In the meantime, the sixth evening brought night's beginning back
again and drove away the light, alternating day and night. While all
breathing creatures sought sweet repose, Adam too felt the release of a
sleep that left his body limp. For the Almighty Father cast over him a
slumber that weighed upon his heart, and the coming of its weight made
his senses sluggish, so that no power could release his sleeping mind.
Even if thunder had happened to crash around his untroubled ears, even
if the heavens had resounded and the sky's vault had been shaken, his
limbs, heavy under God's hand, would not have disturbed that repose.
It was then that God took from among all his bones a single rib, lifting
it from the left side and reforming the flesh. From it arose a form de-
lightful in its grace and beauty, and suddenly woman informed that new
apparition. God joined her to her husband by eternal law and made
good the loss with the fruit their marriage would bear.

That death which Christ, who had Himself taken on a human body,
freely underwent, followed the figurative model of that sleep. As He
who would suffer that death hung high, nailed to a lofty tree, paying for
the sins of the world, a soldier plunged his spear into the side of His
crucified body, and at once a jet leapt from the wound and flowed
down. Even then, the water promised a bath that brings eternal life to
the world and is accompanied by a stream of blood that signifies martyr-
dom. And, in the days that followed, as He lay still for two nights, the
Church rose from His rib and became His bride.

In the very beginning, the Ruler of the world, taking care to sanctify
the symbolic meaning of so powerful a bond, bound the marriage of His
creatures with these words, "Live in harmonious devotion to one an-
other and fill the world. May a long-lived line of children blossom from
this happy seed. Let there be neither number nor limit to the years of
their lives. Progeny I have given you without end, whom you may look
upon forever, you who are appointed first author of the race. May your
great-grandson, scattering the offspring he has raised across the centuries,
still number his own great-grandparents among the living, and may the
offspring of his children lead their own children, themselves rich in
years, before the eyes of their ancestors."

"Thereafter in every age, the venerable law of marriage, will be pre-
served in its own form inviolate by all. Let woman, who was taken
from the body of man, remain faithful in marriage and let another not
separate what God has joined and united. And let the husband, bound
by a righteous love, leave his mother with his father. Let concern for
parents not break those bonds, but let the lives of both man and woman

become bound in one flesh." Linking their promises by an eternal contract in this way, He proclaimed the joyous marriage and made an angel's song resound, note linked with note, in honor of their chaste modesty. Paradise served as their bridal chamber, the world itself was their dowry and the stars above it rejoiced with flames of happiness.

There is a place, Nature, in the eastern precincts of the earth, which has been preserved to hold your deepest secrets. It lies in that land where, at the rising of the sun, the dawn strikes the neighboring Indies as it waxes. The race that lives there now lies beneath the glowing vault of the sky, whose light, burning in the white air, turns them dark. Upon them pure light falls continually, and because of heaven's proximity, their dark bodies preserve the hue of night that birth has given them. But radiant eyes shine in their unkempt bodies with a stolen brightness, and their terrifying aspect grows even clearer when with those fiery eyes they cast their gaze on someone. Their uncombed hair is stiff and pulled straight back so that their receding hairline leaves their foreheads bare. Whatever wonderful product redounds to our benefit the nature of their rich earth has given entire to them. Whatever fragrant or beautiful thing comes to us is from that place. There, the ebony, which shares their color, grows from the pitchy tinder of the earth, and there that mammoth beast gives up its beautiful tusks to provide the world with the gift of ivory. And so, beyond the Indies, where the world begins, where they say the horizon joins earth to heaven, there upon a mountaintop remains a grove inaccessible to all mortals, fenced off by an everlasting boundary after the perpetrator of that original sin fell from grace and was expelled. And when the sinners, as they deserved, were driven from that happy seat, that holy plot of earth received heavenly guardians. There, winter frost never comes, as is the case when the seasons succeed one another, nor, after the cold do the suns of summer return, as when in our land the sky's high circuit brings back the warm season, or, as ice thickens, the fields grow white with frost. There, the mildness of heaven maintains a spring that has no end. No gusty west wind blows there, and ever beneath a clear sky the thinning clouds give way to sunshine. Nor by its nature does the place want for the showers it does not possess, but the buds are content with the gift of their own dew. The entire land flourishes endlessly, and the lovely face of the warm earth remains bright. Grass stands ever upon the hills and leaves upon the trees. Whatever propagates itself blossoms again and again and nurtures its buds with fast-flowing sap. Whatever blooms for us now in the span of a year, there, a mere month's time brings to ripe fruitfulness. There the lilies brighten unwithered by the sun. Its touch does not violate the violets, but a preserving grace bathes their unfailing faces with a rosy blush. And so since there is no winter and torrid summer does not burn, autumn with its crops and spring with blossoms occupy the year entire. There, the cinnamon, which false tradition attributes to the Sabaeans, grows and is gathered by that life-conceiving bird, who, when he perishes in the end that is his birth, burnt in his nest, succeeds himself and arises from the death which he himself sought out. Nor is he content by nature to be born only once, but the long life of his feeble body is renewed, and again and again birth resurrects his old age when it has been consumed by flames. There, the branch that exudes fragrant balsam sends forth from its rich trunk a perpetual flow, and if it happens that a light wind stirs a breeze, then the rich forest, touched by gentle gusts, trembles with a soft rustling of leaves and wholesome flowers, and the wind, when dispersed over the earth, gives off a pleasant fragrance. There, a glimmering fountain rises from a clear pool. Not even in silver does such grace shine, nor will crystal with its cold glitter give forth so much light. At the edge of its banks small green stones flash, and whatever gems the ostentation of this world admires, these, as mere pebbles, lie there too. The fields produce a quilt of color and adorn the landscape with a natural diadem. The river that rises from the gently flowing source of that fountain is quickly divided into four broad streams. Two of them, which mark the long boundary of the Parthian bowman's land with their fixed limit, they call Euphrates and Tigris. The third is Geon, which in Latin is called Nile. It is more noble than the rest, and its headwaters are unknown. Its gentle waves flow into Egypt to enrich its land in the appointed season. For as often as the river swells and its stream bursts over its banks, as often as it flows over the fields with its black silt, the land's fertility is increased in value by the water, and, although the sky is clear, the river's inundation provides a land-borne rain. Then Memphis lies hidden, trapped beneath the broad flood, and the landowner sails above his vanished fields. All boundaries disappear as well. Walls are swamped and levelled as the flood passes its own judgement and puts a stop to the lawsuits that arise each year. The joyful shepherd watches his familiar pasture sink, and in his acre of green meadow, fish swim through the strange water, taking the place of his flocks. But after the flood has fertilized the seeds with its abundant waters and has wed the secret parts of the thirsting earth, the Nile withdraws and regathers its scattered waters. As the lake it formed disappears, it becomes once more a river. Then the ancient barrier of its banks is restored to its channel, and its waves are confined, until finally its divided mouth is scattered over distant wastes as it runs in seven streams to the open sea. But why, Nile, should your source alone be said to lie hidden from the world, for you are not alone of unknown origin? No, you are one of four that pour from that unknown spring, which looks down on all rivers from its high course and, as father of the sea itself, is pre-eminent over all the waters that mountain, plain and clouds disgorge. The fourth river is Physon, which India possesses and calls the Ganges. Whenever it swells at its fragrant source and is set in motion, it glides along, stealing the fallen wealth which the winds scatter in lovely groves and carrying it off along its stream to exile in our land. Both of its banks are bountiful, and just as our rivers are used to carry smooth papyrus and to bring rushes and slender plants downstream, so the mighty Ganges brings with it its rich refuse and gives to the world what it casts from its channel.

Meanwhile, those first blessed creatures, whom the mighty Creator had joined, were settled in their home in Paradise, and the Lord placed their rewards before them with this condition: "O greatest work of your Maker, you whom Our hand alone has made, while all else We ordered into existence by Our word, do you see how this lovely grove with its great abundance serves up to you its countless riches? All these things will be given to you to eat without limit. Seek your nourishment from them. Take the crops that have been given to you and pluck their fruits. Here let your carefree life be tranquil as you enjoy for years and years a sweet pleasure in My creation and its delights. There is, however, in the middle of the grove a tree that you can see and that carries in its seed the knowledge of good and evil. Do not extend to it a touch that is forbidden. Nor, by any chance, let the reckless desire to learn what your teacher forbids overcome you. It is better for those who are blessed to be ignorant of what causes harm when it is examined. I call as witness the earth I made that if anyone eats the forbidden fruit from that tree, he will pay for the bold deed with the hazard of death. I do not speak of an immense obligation, for holding to what is right is easy. He who keeps this command shall have life; he who violates it an end of life." The young couple accepted His command and gladly followed it, promising that His law would be followed for ever. And so, their new natures, ignorant of evil and unaware of guile, instilled in their unsuspecting minds no fear. And God the Father, leaving them in their holy dwelling with these instructions, ascended joyfully into the star-filled court of the sky.

## 2. Original Sin

And so Adam and Eve, perfectly free and without care, with no knowledge of the disaster that would come, made use of their possessions and enjoyed the fertility of Paradise in happiness. From its soil the responsive earth produced abundant food for its lords, and indeed in turn they picked from the tender grass again and again the fruit of some heavily laden bush. And if the trees' branches, bending beneath their fecund weight, let their soft fruits drop from above, then at once the empty branch would begin to burst into flower and put forth growth from its new buds. If the couple sought delight in the enjoyment of sleep, they would lie in a soft meadow on a quilt of grass. Although their sacred grove offered every delight for their pleasure and gave itself to them along with an abundance of fresh foods, nevertheless, they took their meals and sought food in a random way because no hunger compelled them and no empty stomach urged them to fill bodies weary with nourishment. Were it not their pleasure to try the food given them, hunger, which was unknown to them, would have asked for nothing to eat, and no nourishment would have been required to support their life, which was unfailing. They looked upon their naked bodies and felt no shame in beholding each other's limbs. Their simple decency felt nothing unseemly, for the nature of man is not the cause of sin but the cause of his shame. Whatever bodily parts our benevolent Creator formed, our flesh later caused to be filled with shame when it used them. But in that early time the couple's pure minds preserved an unsullied vision. Such a glorious life they say the angels live in their seat in the starry realms, a life like that which Christ promises to restore to the souls of the redeemed after death. For them there will be no desire for marriage, nor will the joining of flesh bring their passionate sexes together in a disgusting union. Moans will cease and with them debauchery, fear, anger, passion, deceit, grief and treachery, along with sadness, quarrelling and spite. No one will be poor, no one greedy, but under a single peace Christ, the glory of the saints, will answer all our needs.

The holy beginnings of human life kept the thoughts and feelings of those first creatures under control with these good things, until, in the first contest, sin overcame them, overpowered as they were by their lying enemy. He had formerly been an angel, but after he had been set aflame by his own sin and burned to accomplish proud deeds of boldness, imagining that he had made himself, that he himself had been his own creator, he conceived a mad fury in his raging heart and denied his

own author. "I shall acquire," he said, "a name divine and shall estab-
lish my eternal abode higher than Heaven's vault, I, who will be like
God on high and not unequal to His mightiest power." As he boasted
in this way, Power pre-eminent threw him from Heaven and took from
the exile his ancient honor. He who had been brilliant and who had
held the first rank among creatures paid the first penalties under the ver-
dict of the Judge who was to come. Quite appropriately, a more severe
sentence punished the kind of creature whose fall you would consider
remarkable, for the perpetrator makes his own crime the more grievous.
For the obscure sinner the guilt is less, but the evil is considered graver
if someone more exalted commits it. However, insofar as that fallen an-
gel penetrates with his keen senses even into what is hidden, insofar as
he sees the future and unlocks the secrets of the world, the brilliant na-
ture of his angelic power endures. This is a portent dreadful to speak of
but known by the traces of his work, for whatever dire deed is commit-
ted anywhere on earth it is he who instructs the hand of crime and
guides its weapons. He, the unseen thief, wages his battles through pub-
lic acts of criminality. Often altering his appearance in this way and
that, he puts on as a disguise now the face of men, now the savage visage
of beasts. At times he will become all at once a counterfeit vision of a
winged bird and feign again a virtuous mien. Or, appearing as a girl
with a lovely body, he draws men's passionate gazes toward obscene
joys. And often, for greedy men he will even shine as heaps of silver and
fire their minds with the love of imagined gold. Then, once touched, he
flees from the deluded fools, an empty fantasy. For in none of his shapes
can one find abiding constancy or grace, but in whatever way he seizes
and holds a man to do him harm, masking his real face, he assumes an
outward visage fit for guile and suited to secret deceit. And even greater
power than this has been granted to this savage creature to make himself
appear holy. So it happened that Nature, which the Creator built true
and bestowed upon the man he had created, remained sound for a while,
but in time this creature bent on ruin turned it to his own depraved uses.

When this scoundrel saw those human beings, newly created, leading
a happy life and free of danger in their peaceful abode, commanding an
obedient world under the law they had accepted and enjoying their sub-
ject realm amid tranquil joys, a spark of jealousy produced a sudden
ardor in his breast and his seething malice rose to a violent boil. He
then happened to be nearby, in the place to which he had fallen, plung-
ing from Heaven and dragging with him along a precipitous course his
confederate band. Taking stock of the situation and pressing to his heart

the outrage of his recent fall, he grieved all the more that he had lost what another had won. Then his shame, mixed with gall, released the grumbling from his breast and gave his plaintive sighs release. "O, that this upstart concoction should arise in our place and that a hated race take its rise from our destruction! My valor kept me in high station, but now, behold, I am rejected and driven forth, and this clay succeeds to my angelic honors. Earth now possesses Heaven. The very soil, exalted in this base construction, now rules, and power passes from us and is lost. And yet, it is not totally lost. A great part retains its native strength and must be reckoned with for its great capacity to do harm. No use delaying. Even now I shall meet them in a contest of seduction, now while the security of these first days and a simplicity ignorant of guile lays them open to my weapons. They will be better caught by treachery while they are alone, before they send their fecund offspring forth to fill unending ages yet to come. The earth must be allowed to produce nothing immortal. Rather let the source of this race perish, and the casting out of its own fallen sire will be the seed of its own death. Let the very beginning of its life bring forth the peril of death. Let all be stricken in this one creature, for when the root is killed it will produce no life in the branches above. This solace alone remains for me in my exile. If I am not able to scale Heaven once again, since it has been barred, let it be barred to these creatures as well. We must consider our own fall less dire if this new substance is destroyed by a like misfortune. Let him be the companion of our fall. Let him endure a partnership in punishment. Let him share with us the flames that even now I can see. Nor will the way to deceive him be difficult to find. I must show him the same path which not long ago I freely followed in my own headlong fall. The same pride which drove me from that kingdom will drive man from the threshold of Paradise." So he spoke, and then the groaning of that anguished creature put a stop to his words.

Now the serpent happened to be a creature superior to all others in guile, whose cunning heart burned with envy. Among all the animals, it was his form that the transgressor chose to assume, circling his aerial body with skin. He stretched himself out and was transformed in an instant into the snake, becoming himself the long-necked reptile. He picked out his brilliant neck with spots, made rough the coils of his smooth tail and armed his back with rigid scales. In just this shape, as spring begins and the early months of the hot season send us warmth as a happy harbinger after days of congealed ice, the snake, emerging from the old year and shaking his slippery length awake, strips the brittle skin from its gleaming body and slips forth, leaving the secret places of the earth, and his terrible shape bears a frightening beauty. Terrifying is the flash in his eyes, whose keen vision rejoices as it learns to accustom itself to the sun it longed for. Now he makes himself out to be alluring by giving play to his mouth with whisper after whisper or by thrusting his triple tongue from his throat.

Well then, when the deceiver with his seductive treachery had put on the serpent's form and had insinuated himself throughout the entire snake, he hastened to the grove where the happy young people happened to be plucking red apples from a green branch. Then the serpent, afraid that he might not be able, because of the man's steadfast mind, to turn his heart to evil with his dose of poison, stretched his creeping coils out atop a tall tree, and fitting his length to its highest branches, began to pester the weaker ear with a whisper. "O happy creature and glory of the earth, maiden most beautiful, you whom a radiant grace decks with the blush of modesty, you who will become the parent of the race, whom the vast world looks to as mother, you, the first and faithful delight, the solace of your husband, without whom he, although greater, could not live, rightly your sweet spouse is subject to your love, he for whom you will produce offspring in accordance with your pledge. To you a worthy dwelling place has been granted on this summit of Paradise. The substance of the world is subject to you, is your servant and trembles before you. Whatever heaven or earth creates, whatever the sea in its great gulf produces is bestowed upon you for your use. Nature denies you nothing. See how power over everything is granted to you. Nor am I jealous but rather astonished that your otherwise unhampered touch refrains from one sweet tree among all the others. I would like to know who gives such a dreadful command, who begrudges such gifts and mingles want with wealth." And so with evil intent, his hissing feigned flattering words. What stupidity, woman, clouded your mind? Did you feel no shame in speaking with the serpent, conversing with the brute, when that beast assumed your speech? Did you tolerate the monster and reply to it as well?

Then when Eve, who was open to seduction, had heard the deadly poison and approved the evil praise, she spoke to the serpent with shallow words. "Sweet serpent, potent with your delightful words, God did not, as you think, urge hunger upon us or forbid us to refresh our bodies with every kind of nourishment. Behold, you can see the banquets the whole world provides for us. Our generous Father has given us all these for our lawful use and has given us free rein over our lives.

That tree alone which you see in the middle of the grove is forbidden as food, and touching its fruit is the only thing we may not enjoy. Our rich and varied meals, however, partake of everything else. But if we violate this law with criminal license, our Creator swore and predicted in a frightening voice that we would at once pay the penalty of something called death. What He calls death, do you now, wise serpent, graciously explain, since it is a thing unknown to us in our simplicity."

Then the shrewd snake, teacher of death, gladly instructed her in destruction and addressed these words to the ears he had captivated. "Woman, you fear a word that holds no terror. No sentence of swift death will fall upon you. No, the Father in His jealousy has not allotted to you a portion equal to His. He has not given to you the understanding of these high matters which He keeps to Himself. What joy can there be in seeing and apprehending this lovely world while your blind minds are shut up in a miserable prison? This is the way Nature creates the gross senses and wide eyes of animals. If your powers are the same, a single sun serves all, and human vision is no different from a beast's. But take my advice instead. Fix your mind on things celestial and turn your mental powers, once lifted up, heavenward. This fruit you fear to touch because it is forbidden will give you knowledge of whatever your Father lays away as secret. Whatever you do, don't withhold your touch in hesitation now. Don't let your captive joy be bridled by this law any longer, for when you have tasted the divine savor on your lips, your eyes will soon become clear and make your vision equal to that of gods, in knowing what is holy as well as what is evil, in distinguishing between right and wrong, truth and falsehood."

The woman, too ready to believe, put on a submissive look and admired him as, in a dissembling whisper, he promised gifts like these. And even now she began to hesitate more and waver, began to apply her doubting mind increasingly to death. When he saw that she had lost the struggle and that the crisis was approaching, he referred again to the name "gods" and their pre-eminence and drew one of the apples from the deadly tree, bathing its beauty in a pleasant fragrance. He extolled its appearance and offered it to Eve, who bent her head ever so hesitantly above it. Nor did the woman, perversely gullible as she was, spurn the wretched gift, but she took the deadly apple from him and held it in her hand. Without further prompting she brought it to her flared nostrils and parted her lips, as in her ignorance, she played with the death that was to come.

O how often, stung by conscience, did she withdraw it from her lips

and how often did her right hand, faltering beneath the weight of her
own daring wickedness, yield and, trembling, flee from committing the
crime! And yet, she wanted to be like the gods, and that ambition's nox-
ious poison stole through her. Opposites took hold of her mind. On
one side tugged her longing, on the other her fear. Her pride dashed it-
self against the law and yet, even as it did, the law came to her aid. The
alternating surges of her divided heart seethed, as this harsh battle with
self took place, but the serpent, who had kindled her desire, did not put
aside his deception. He continued to display the food even as she hesitat-
ed, complaining of her delay, and the woman, tottering on the brink of
her own imminent destruction, aided his endeavor.

But when the doomed woman's fatal judgement settled on indulging
that eternal hunger with the fruit of sin and of satisfying the serpent by
eating the food she took from him, she gave in to his treachery and, her-
self consumed, bit into the apple. The sweet venom entered her body,
and she caught with the bite horrid death. The shrewd snake held back
his joy at first, and cruel victory hid its savage triumph.

Adam, ignorant of what she had done, was joyfully making his way
back from another part of the grove through the wide fields and pasture-
lands. He was yearning for his wife's embrace and chaste kisses. The
woman came to meet him, since daring then stirred the female madness
in her spirited breast for the first time. This is the way she began to
speak, carrying the deadly apple, half-eaten, keeping it for her poor hus-
band. "Sweet spouse," she said, "take this food from the branch of life;
perhaps it will make you like the almighty Thunderer, equal to the
gods. I do not bring you this gift in ignorance but having just now ac-
quired new wisdom. The first taste has reached my stomach and has
boldly, dangerously broken our covenant with the Lord. Give me your
trust ungrudgingly, for it is wrong for a man's mind to hesitate over
what I, a woman, could do. Perhaps you were afraid to take the lead;
well then, follow at least and lift up your abject spirit. Why do you turn
your eyes? Why do you put off desires that will bring you good? Why
do you rob yourself so long of the honor that is to come?"

When she had spoken, she gave him the food of death, the con-
queror to be, and as sin nourished their death, their souls perished. The
unlucky man listened to her words, that whisper tempting him to evil,
and then finally dashed the good sense that those words had perverted.
The anxiety that follows trembling fear did not shake him, nor did he
hesitate, as the woman had, over the first bite. Rather, he was quick to
follow and, firm in his infirmity, grasped the poison dowry from the

lips of his poor spouse and brought the noxious food toward his opened
jaw. Scarcely had his horrid maw taken a single bite of the apple,
scarcely had the food released its first faint flavor, when, behold, a sud-
den brilliance played about his face and scattered strange visions around
him with its mournful light. It was not Nature, you see, that caused
blindness in mankind. No, our perfect species did not bring forth faces
deprived of the use of light. But rather now, Adam, you will be blind,
you who were not satisfied to know what your Almighty Creator
wanted you to know. The power of sight was created for you for use in
life, but now, by your own choice, you will look upon death as well.
Then the couple lamented the opening of their eyes, for the sin of dis-
obedience shone forth, and their bodies felt their own indecent impulses.
Their shame, at once extinguished or perhaps new born—for I am not
sure how to put it—beheld for the first time their naked limbs. Their
minds, conscious of their own sin, blushed, and the law of the flesh,
which was now imposed on their members, struggled within them.

It was from that act that their posterity, because of their tainted seed,
conceived a desire to learn the future through unlawful arts, to direct
their dull senses toward holy secrets, to search out what Heaven holds
on high or what is sunk in the foul depths of the earth, and to break the
careful laws of nature, now to inquire from the stars under what constel-
lation each man is born and how prosperous he may be for the remain-
der of his life, and to predict different outcomes although the signs are
the same, to assign because of opposite motions a different lot to twins
who are born at the same time and whom a single birth brings into the
light of day, finally to relate to the stars certain local divinities whom a
younger age placed in the Heaven of antiquity and to arrange empty
names in the measureless sky in honor of those long since buried in in-
fernal night.

Now who has the power to explain properly the deception of magic,
which makes trial of occult forces for a heart that remains silent, which
longs to be united with powers divine? Once upon a time the prophet
and lawgiver Moses, when he was under the rule of Egypt's proud king
and was showing the strange miracles which had been ordered as signs,
so provoked the jealousy of the priests of that land that they attempted
similar things and thereby, owing to their own burning zeal, heaped up
even greater ruin for themselves. If they had rightly possessed the power
to help, then they would have been quick to remove and not to add
other portents. But their anger, able to compete in portents but no
match in power, appropriately repeated what it could not eliminate.

This is in fact the source of the Marsians' power too, whose crime is applauded, when with their silent art they make fierce snakes appear from afar and bid the vipers time and time again to assail them. Then, when each sees that his snake is stirred to combat and recognizes that the ears of the stubborn serpent are closed to all other sounds, he strikes up within himself the secret chant that is his shield. At the sound of the spell-binding words, the snake's poison grows weak at once, and before long the harmless creature can be handled without danger. Then only the bite, not the venom need be feared, although there are occasions when a man perishes while singing his incantation, if it happens that the snake is deaf and hence spurns the ingenious mumbling of the charmer. Since it is from their mother Eve and the very origin of their being that these magicians draw this skill at snake-charming and speech, they are even able to engage in conversations in song. At the same time, however, another care, which is at odds with their own well-being, agitates them, for they are troubled by foreknowledge of the ends of their own lives. They imagine, you see, that they converse with shades summoned from the world below and gain information from them as well. Fools, for a spirit of error, which raves inside them, gives replies to their inquiries that are devoid of significance. But so as not to string out the tale of many individual cases, suffice it to say that whoever attempts to understand what is forbidden will be made a mockery of today and condemned by a judgement that is eternal.

Eve was not, of course, the only searcher after evil. I shall now tell of another woman, who, as she struggled with a similar moral infection, was not able, although at his side, to overcome her own Adam. A passion for sin had set afire certain cities, loosening the reins of morality and countenancing civic criminality. Lewdness became the law, desire took every right for its own and passion, after striding across the capital of the realm, held the native people beneath a tyranny of the flesh. In their eagerness for sin, which the government of the place proposed to the trusting populace, who had been for a long time all too ready to obey, all of them believed that it was wrong to abstain and shameful not to sin, for each sin they committed bound them more closely together. When the Judge and Ruler of the world, offended by such deeds, became enraged and made ready flames and an end for the place, He spoke to Lot, alone of all those many people, Lot, a man unlike the others, in his house by himself, by then a stranger in his own city. "These towns long filled with lascivious madness bespatter Heaven itself with stains and tire Our ears, closed though they are, with the clamor of their sins.

Destruction hangs over them; the land, aflame with guilt, will glow with
fire, and a storm of lightning will blot out this seething pot of crime
which weeping has not extinguished. The very earth will be reduced to
undying embers, which, even after the conflagration, will preserve their
own living ashes and form a soil such that, if it is but lightly trodden
upon, its colorless surface will flee and draw away at the least touch.
Leave your house now and forsake this land that is doomed. Let these
guilty fields sink down with the inhabitants who deserve it, and let not
the death that hangs over them join you with those with whom life did
not join you. Let your spouse be your solace and leave this place con-
tent with that companionship alone. Speed your flight, take a direct
path and let neither of you look back at the cities that are to be de-
stroyed. Be ignorant of the evil. Let those who have deserved it pay the
penalty and let anyone who turns back look upon the sight of his own
death with them, but let terror not afflict the righteous." So their Father
spoke, and they hastened to depart from the land, made an end to delay
and left its cruel fields behind.

Now the sky, choked by thick smoke, began to be hidden and to
send forth a rumbling such as had never been heard before. It was not
as when air troubled by frequent thunder displays harmless bolts to the
frightened earth. No, this final calamity sent ghastly signs straight
through the confused atmosphere with a menacing whine. As this was
happening, the couple who had been forewarned were already on their
way, in obedience to their Maker's commands, and without turning
their faces, were heading toward the safe haven that had been granted
them. But the shrewd serpent, wanting to play the hero and accustomed
since his destruction of Eve to touching a woman's mind, stirred with
his coaxing a desire in Lot's wife to witness the ruin and catch sight of
the death she had escaped, for here too he was afraid to make trial of the
man's spirit. O the madness of her mind! Why is it not enough for one
woman to have succumbed to his guile? We know now that he who has
knowledge of evil has forsaken the portion of the righteous. This is the
reason: if the examples of our parents fail to terrify, then you will be-
come an example for our fear, woman, and after you the awful desire to
know what is hidden may vanish, for looking upon what it is unlawful
to know or forbidden to see, you will do nothing more than look back
and then be unable report what you see.

Then, when the woman heard a louder uproar from the nearby city,
she turned her face back and, almost at the very first glance, grew still.
Her motion was checked and she ceased in an instant to look upon the

scene. Then her blood congealed and the rigidity of marble suffused her body. Her cheeks grew stiff and a strange pallor touched her face. She did not close her eyes nor fall with the weight with which a lifeless corpse strikes the earth, but stood as a block of stone, glowing with a fearful light. Her captive appearance remained solid and unchanging, and so you would not easily be able to tell whether the creature had turned to glass or stone or metal, did you not taste the salt on your lips. Thereupon this woman, overcome by her own insipid crime, grew sharper in spite of her lack of wit, she who can sting our senses and preserve with the salt of her example those who see her. In this case, however, it is important to note that her husband was not seduced, that her brave Adam did not follow his spouse and was not overcome. And indeed I am the readier to believe this because his wife did not come to him and tell her story. For if she had reported what she had discovered, perhaps she might have persuaded him to disregard God's commands by looking back, just as that reckless heroine of long ago did when she made her spouse taste the apple, she who, after betraying herself, betrayed her mate as well and dealt a blow to descendants yet unborn.

Then the victorious serpent, rejoicing in his contest with Eve and shaking the ruddy crest on his scaly head, no longer disguised the triumph which he had kept to himself earlier, but with even greater bitterness he taunted the vanquished couple and began to speak. "Behold, the godlike glory of the praise I promised abides with you. Whatever knowledge was within my grasp, trust now that it is yours. I have shown you everything, have guided your senses through what was hidden, and whatever evil ingenious nature had denied to you, this I have taught, allowing man to join left and right, foul and fitting. And so your fate is sealed forever and I have consecrated you to myself. Nor does God, although He formed you earlier, have greater rights in you. Let Him hold what He Himself made. What I taught is mine, and the greater portion remains with me. You owe much to your Creator but more to your teacher." So he spoke and, leaving them trembling in a veil of smoke, his counterfeit body fled through the clouds and vanished.

## 3. God's Judgement

It was the hour when the sinking sun, after crossing the midpoint of heaven's vault and leaving behind the apex of its central arc, bathes the earth with light breezes as night draws near. But for Adam and Eve a greater wave of anxiety rolled in, and a seething anguish took hold of their hearts, conscious as they were of sin. Now that their senses were captive, shame turned their eyes aside and made repugnant the sight of one another's bodies. Since they might no longer gaze with untroubled vision at the flesh now marked with the stain that their sin had placed on it, they searched for clothes and sought to cover their limbs with pliant foliage, and as a result laid bare their wickedness by wearing clothes.

Nearby stood a fig tree with shady branches, all covered with verdant foliage. Taking a moist strip from the bark he had peeled from that tree, Adam began at once to sew leaves on it. With this green garment he eased his shame, and the pitiful woman clothed herself with similar skill. Those whom a treacherous madness had fed with that unfortunate apple, the same madness now clothed with a leaf. Those whom it had rendered naked because of that other cruel tree, it also covered with the oppressive weight of a slender sapling. And yet, the time will come when a new Adam will heal and cleanse the sin of one tree by means of yet another tree, when He will make that same substance by which death prevailed a medicine of life, and Death, you will be destroyed by death. A brazen serpent will one day hang from another lofty branch and, although it represents a poisonous creature, will wash away all poison and destroy the ancient snake with its own form.

Now the Creator, amid the tender foliage of that verdant grove, was gathering from the bright sky winds moist with dew. At once both the man and the woman, as they listened in awe, sensed the presence of the Lord. Then, in that sad and detested light, they grew afraid that the day would bear witness to their newly discovered sin. If by chance a pit with vast caverns had spread open for them or if the earth had shown them a sudden crevice, they would not have been reluctant, as they stood there trembling, to hurl themselves into these with a headlong leap. And if a sentence of death had even then been pronounced, concern for alleviating their shame would have grasped even at that. They would have given themselves up to flame or flood, or their right hands, as their judges, would have plunged a sword into their breasts, inflicting an unmerciful wound. This is how much the poor couple longed for death the moment they deserved it, in spite of the fact that it was not yet known to them from their own peril. For the very beginnings of things mark their ends and foretell the approach of a corresponding grief. So it will be when the final age consumes the feeble world, when a sudden flash strikes everything and mankind hears the blaring of Heaven's trumpet with which the herald will frighten the terrified earth with the message of the Judge's coming. So it will be when the divine Shepherd separates the sheep who are pure, when the goats, which are of another hue, are put in a place apart, and when chaos acts as a barrier between them, and a whirlpool with rolling swells of fire fills it with waves of brimstone. So it will be when there spreads out before mankind the lake of flames from which, they say, the boiling clouds of Sodom, gathering like a thunderhead, once poured bolts of lightening like raindrops upon that place's sins, as foul night rained fire, and on all sides men's deaths fell dripping from the sky through the fervid air. This was the way that grim rivulets gushed out of the fiery font of Gehenna on an alien age. But in that frightful hour that is to come, whatever man the Judge sentences to live after death and burn in everlasting punishment, him a heavier doom than Gehenna's will snatch from the death he desires. Although it would be better for the body, its limbs scattered, to sleep a perpetual sleep in unyielding death, nevertheless the urn will vomit them all forth, all those unwilling souls for whom there is but one desire: to die again and escape the awareness of their pain. But the flame of the glowing furnace will receive them and consume them in its fires as a food that is never exhausted.

Now that first young couple, struggling in vain, were rushing through lonely wastelands in the belief that their deeds might be hidden by some foolproof deception, in the hope that they had escaped notice in the dark shadows around them. Unhappy creatures, what good is this? Do you turn your eyes from the Judge? The Judge sees you all the same. And why are you unwilling to look upon Him when you are clearly seen? He does not darken the lovely sun if someone casts his eyes down in fear of its blinding brilliance, if his sickly vision cannot endure the robust circle of its light. Then God, who knew where the man was, started to rebuke and question poor Adam in a frightening voice. And Adam, summoning from his frightened breast a few trembling words, made but this brief reply: "Terror of You, heavenly Father, settling upon our minds, drove us to seek concealment, for, because my body was naked and my limbs uncovered, I was, I confess, ashamed and fled from the light of the sky through these hidden wastes."

"And who," God asked, "struck this sudden shame into your heart? Whence comes this new vision? But a little while ago neither skins nor woven garments covered you with their protection. Your pristine form, better satisfied with its own grace, was pleasing in your eyes. But, after our covenant had been broken, after your taste touched the forbidden fruit, nature's covering alone was not enough for you, and to that extent nakedness presents itself to the naked, because a disgusting urge tries to prove your bodies foul."

Adam, when he saw himself clearly convicted, and when the Lord's just account had revealed the full extent of his guilt, did not with humble prayers ask forgiveness for his sin; he did not beg with promises or weeping, nor did a confession on bended knee anticipate his just punishment with a defendant's tears. Now, pitiful himself, he was not yet worthy of pity, for his pride, roused by the consciousness of his sin and further stirred by his own haughty complaints, was at last unleashed and launched into this mad speech. "Alas, this woman, evilly married to accomplish the destruction of her spouse, she whom You gave to me, poor man, as companion under Your very first law, she, once destroyed herself, destroyed me with her wicked counsel. She persuaded me to take the apple whose taste she already knew. The woman is the source of this evil and the guilt arises from her. I was too believing, but then, You taught me to believe, giving me marriage and weaving these sweet bonds. Would that the happy unwed life that once flourished for me were mine and would that I had never tasted wedlock and become subject to this depraved companion!"

Then the Creator, provoked by Adam's stubbornness, solemnly addressed Eve as she grieved. "Why, as you fell, did you drag your poor spouse down? Not satisfied, treacherous woman, with your own fall, did you indeed cast his masculine good sense down from the high safe place that was its dwelling?" She, in her shame, her cheeks suffused with an unhappy blush, cried that she had been deceived, that the snake was the author of her crime, he who had persuaded her to taste the apple with a bite that had been forbidden.

Then, when she had finished, God's sentence made clear His final decree, and with His first words He branded the snake guilty. "You, snake, by whose deceit the woman sinned and herself delivered up her husband as a companion in error, for the crime of each you are responsible and will pay the penalty for what each did. You shall not stand erect in head and body, but prone, you shall wheel your cunning heart across the earth, and so that your sinuous coils may run trembling and in flight, not walking but slipping along with twisting spasms, self will creep behind self and living chains will bind your wriggling form. Then, in return for the food you urged upon these poor creatures, eating earth, you will enjoy an empty repast, and for those months I designate, driven from the world above and enclosed in the earth, you shall be without the sun that shines on all. Among all the animals that now fill the earth you will be the author of death, will become for all a deadly horror. And in a special way the unhappy woman, as her hatred of you persists, will with her future offspring balance the account of hostility in such a way that seed will commit to seed the promise of revenge. You will always wait stubbornly upon the frightened woman's heel, and I decree that she will at last crush your head and overcome the one who overcame her."

Next the Judge directed His wrath toward Eve, who was stricken with awe: "But you, woman, who disobeyed My first law, hear what kind of life remains for the remainder of your days. You will endure the domination of your husband in bed and fear your lord, whom I had given you as a mate. In subjection you will obey his commands and with bent head accustom yourself to his male pleasures. Soon, when your womb conceives and feels the growing life within it, you will testify to its burden with groans, and your uneasy belly will carry closed within you its growing load until, when the allotted time has passed, and your weariness is complete, an offspring, producing life, makes good nature's curse with the vengeance birth takes. This will be a parent's punishment. And why should I speak now of the many different perils of motherhood in years to come? For when, woman, wearied with hard work, you have brought forth the child you longed for, giving birth in the manner I have described, it will sometimes happen that a child will be taken from you and you will weep for your meaningless suffering."

Meanwhile, Adam in his fear had been bracing himself for some time against what the Lord's terrible judgement would at last hold in store for him. And to him the Father spoke: "Now listen carefully and hear what you have earned, you whom this fickle woman has overpowered. Previously the earth, with its lovely blooms, was without stain, but it will no longer be as reliable, no longer remain simple and bear seeds untainted, nor will it show its old lifeless surface throughout a world that is now corrupt. Following your example, the earth will be ever rebellious and, armed with brambles and thorns, will learn to resist your efforts. And if it yields, if it succumbs to the sod-breaking plough and is subdued by the steady biting tooth of the share, still the rich cultivated land will deceive you with treacherous crops. For you will grieve that in the place of wheat weedy grass grows along with crops that are sham and barren stalks. And so, grudgingly your acres will produce the bread you extort from them, bread which your hunger, struggling and sweating all the time, will consume. Let the food, with its own sentence of toil, demand satisfaction for the delight of your recent meal. This food

will make your life like that of the beasts, for as soon as you seek the
juice of herbs and solid nourishment, your stomach will grow heavy
with the weight of a similar excrement. Under conditions like these, a
long period of suffering will roll on until the years assign the end that
is prescribed for you, until in time your limbs, which are compacted of
clay, decay. Formed as you were from mud, you will be reduced again
to earth. Before your own death, however, you will behold your chil-
dren die before you and see in your children your own punishment; this
so that the fearful image of death may be better discerned by you and so
that you may recognize what it is to have sinned, what it is to lament
the dead, what it is to die. And lest by some chance you should escape
any evil which the corrupt world brings forth for those who require
punishment, an even more bitter wrath will be mingled with your al-
ready immeasurable grief, for when your youth begets children, vora-
cious envy will do battle within the world's narrow confines, and
thereafter the globe in all its empty expanse will not be large enough to
satisfy it. The whole earth will be made narrow by two brothers. The
one will rise up to murder the other and stain the new earth with kin-
dred blood. Subsequently, your posterity, who will endure all kinds of
toil, will pay the debt of mortality in disasters of every kind until the
end draws near and dissolves the aged world. Then I command that all
that lives must die and the end of things confute their beginnings." So
He spoke and the earth in terror heard him and quaked.

Then their almighty Father took the hides of goats and clothed the
man and woman and drove them from the holy seat of Paradise. They
fell down to the earth below and entered the empty world together.
Darting here and there, they explored the whole place, and although
they found it dappled with various blossoms and with grass, although it
displayed green meadows and fountains and rivers, to them the appear-
ance of the earth seemed ugly after yours, O Paradise. As they looked
upon it, the whole place struck them as dreadful and, as is the way with
men, what had been lost was what they longed for all the more. The
land grew narrow as they groaned over the confined world around
them. They could not see the end of that world and yet it pressed in on
them. The sky itself grew filthy, and even as they stood beneath the sun,
they convinced themselves that its light had been withdrawn. The stars
that hung in the remotest sky seemed to groan, and heaven's vault
which they had been able to touch before now could scarcely be seen.

Then, surrounded by anxiety and confused by the bitterness of their
grief, they experienced a new emotion. Weeping shook their breasts and

stirred a flood of tears, something unknown to them until then. Unbidden, the droplets flowed down their sensitive cheeks. In the same way our living spirit, disappointed and deprived of its body's frame, when in the fullness of time the end has come, grieves for its sins after death. Then it recalls whatever injustice it committed. Then all the lapses into sin, the transgressions it condemns itself, cause it pain. And if an opportunity to relive its past life could be restored to it, it would willingly bear whatever toils such a contract would impose.

Saint Luke tells the story of a certain rich man whom life pampered as it destroyed him with too much luxury. Proud in his gems and brilliant in his golden jewelry, he double dyed his silken robes in purple. Then when the season enticed him to a bacchanalian feast, the courses, which all the world sent, ran on and on. Whenever some far-off storehouse sent him a delicacy, the vintage Falernian would bubble from his chilled crystal. And what was more, the pungent odor of cinnamon mingled with his incense, and his entire house was fragrant with the fumes of rich balsam. As the burdened tables tottered, whatever the sea or earth creates, whatever rivers bring forth, his pale and weary butler, golden plate in hand, eagerly brought to him from every side. Now it happened that at that time a sick beggar lay before the rich man's gate, his body palsied, his limbs withered. A suppliant, he was begging for help, not in search of gifts but of the leavings of the table only, if it happened that the rich man's superfluity cast anything away. Expecting these, his hungry stomach made its plea. But the rich man gave no ear to his cries and did not, as common decency would require, pay any attention to the sick and destitute creature. Nor did anyone offer for the poor man's sustenance the leftover food that fell from the banquet table when the meal was done. What was more, the face of the sick man was despised and his ulcerous wounds produced only disgust. Indeed, although dogs licked the man's sores with gentle tongues and provided for him, as he grew weak, a savage soothing, the mind of man alone remained ever hard and knew not how to be moved with pity. While all of this happened in accordance with the utterly different fates of each, the death that hung over them struck both men in the same hour. The rich man, who had never imagined it possible, died first. The poor man achieved with difficulty and after a long time the death he desired and in his moment of victory left behind his sickness and his limbs. The rich man, who had for some years lived the good life in his towering castle, was carried to the grave surrounded by the weeping of a crowded funeral procession and his body was given burial in a golden vault. Precious

linens were draped over the towering marble sculpture of his tomb, but
before long his spirit, which had been despatched to the hidden depths
of Avernus, fell to its eternal punishment of cruel flames. Not far away
(so at least it seemed, but as the end of the story shows, it *was* far away)
he saw the beggar, now placed in his heavenly home and rejoicing in the
bosom of Abraham the just, his face utterly changed and not at all like
that of the man whom not long ago they had brought out on the fourth
day after his death, the man whom some grudging gravedigger, his nose
bound up, placed as he was then, covered with but a thin protection of
torn rags, in the unmarked earth, lest the body, decaying as nature's
laws require, spread dread contagion throughout the crowded city.
Then, lifted up to heaven by the hands of angels, he was made rich and
whole again. On the other hand, the dry throat of the proud man, who
had possessed heaps of wealth and had grown dissolute because of his
great riches, cried out for but a drop of water among the flames.

"O Father," he called, "You who in your blessed seat gather the
chosen souls and give rewards to the just who merit them, I realize that
I do not deserve such treatment, but one thing alone I pray for. Send me
Lazarus, have him bring to these burning lips water drawn from there
on his finger. Let him with his cooling touch, if not completely extin-
guish, at least for a time relieve this infernal heat, so that in that brief in-
terval of rest my weary body may gather a fresh breath." As he made
this plea, mingling tears with his screams, the great-souled Patriarch at
long last rebuked him. "Stop this useless gush of words that come too
late, stop these empty prayers of yours. This was not the way you spoke
recently when, as you dined, this man lay at your door, ignored, poor,
sick, hungry and lifeless. In spite of the fact that your table was almost
too small for the heap of your delicacies, nevertheless, a poor man's cry
could not reach your ears. This is the reason why, weighed in the bal-
ance of truth, you have lost claim to the lot of your former life. Now,
I order each of you to suffer a reversal of fates. As for you, be satisfied
now that you possessed a superfluity of wealth then, and let him who
grieved over his original state take joy in the end of his woes. Now
there is no limit to your suffering beyond this. Rather, a boundary,
which runs along a frightening track and cuts off the chaos opposite us
with a wide chasm, does not permit the joining of places separated by
divine covenant and forever forbids all access to you who are damned
just as it does to the souls here."

The rich man continued to groan and again and again made his
prayer in vain. "If it helps not at all to confess my deeds after death and

if your judgement and its immutable terms cannot be changed, then grant me this, a thing forbidden by no law. When I departed from the light, I left five brothers behind me at home. Let him be sent, I beg, to them so that he can admonish them while they are alive, before, set free of the flesh, they fall into torments such as these. For although their hearts are hard and they persist in their rebellion, if someone returns from beyond the barrier of death, they will believe him, since he has experience, and shudder at the prospect of their punishments." But in making even this request, he achieved no result. To us, however, while life is ours and we flourish in the sunlight, the message of Adam who died long ago, brings terror, and brings it while we still have the opportunity to weep, while we may pray for what is not unlawful, while the door we beat at does not carry unyielding bolts.

Observe how everyone understands why that first man wept, he who, when driven from his original home, did not know how to return. For he had endured a kind of death in his fall and could regain his loss with neither prayers nor tears. From that moment his former life, falling back little by little, began to recede, and the power in evil forces was unleashed. Then grim diseases and all kinds of grief drew near. Then the earth grew so rotten in its dreadful abundance that it poured forth fruits with deadly juices. For the same reason savage beasts grew fierce, and for the first time an awareness of their power stirred those once tame to attack, to use their claws and teeth, hooves and horns as weapons. Then the very elements broke nature's laws and all struggled to violate man's trust. The sea swelled under the wind and waves began to roll toward the shore, as the deep was stirred and grew big with a strange surge. Then, for the first time, from a sky covered with foul mist, clouds unleashed upon the frightened world storms of hail, to chastise the thankless labors of man. This heavenly discord begrudged the earth its blossoms and what was more, the earth, turning deceitful and increasingly at war with itself, rejected the bright power of the seeds it received.

The two first-formed creatures experienced all this for the first time, but in time to come how great a price in suffering would their posterity pay! If you had a hundred tongues or an iron voice, you could not enumerate their suffering, not even if the poets, Homer or he whom Mantua gave to the world, were to come to your aid, singing of them each in his own language. Who could recount such upheavals, who in words describe the storms which would churn the ages yet to come? Arms rage, the earth is shaken again and again by fear, streams of blood are spilled, and yet they thirst for more. Why should I speak of the towering cities built by communities of famous men only to be reduced to wasteland, of nations scattered by the ravages of pillaging tribes, of the laying waste, part by part, of the torn earth, of lords reduced to slavery and slaves set in turn over their lords, of the fact that fate's earlier grant of famous lineage often perishes in the lottery of war? And if it happens that there is a lull in the warfare for a short time, need I mention that suits armed with laws foment wild contention, that ambiguous legal claims do battle in the courts, where the disputes of brothers land no lighter blows with oaths than wars land with weapons? But who would pay attention to the oaths defendants take when the criminals' deeds themselves cry out? Who would worry about mere fraud and theft when wholesale plunder rejoices? Who would weep for lesser crimes when not even the greatest can be dealt with? And yet, they are only thought lesser when they are compared to the greatest offenses, and, after all, no crime, when rightly judged, is in itself small. It is not, however, important to review all these things in verse, and so, in this short passage, I shall merely state that, after our ancestors' loss, there was no evil that the world, filled at once with crime and toil, did not either commit or endure, and this although mankind experienced danger in taking risks and guilt in its deeds.

But You Christ, our powerful Lord, You Who are always ready to forgive, You, like the potter, are able to repair the fallen vessel and reshape the dish long broken and in pieces. You find the drachma long hidden in the dirt by lighting lamps with the power of Your word. You are the shepherd who deigns to run and search for the sheep that has left the fold and is wandering in unseemly confusion. You carry it back rejoicing to restore it to its own flock. And so the creature that had been Your care becomes Your burden. So it was that that famous younger son, after he had squandered and depleted all his resources, after his prodigal life had been changed by the using up of all his wealth, was reduced as he deserved to begging for the foul food of pigs and longed to fill his stomach with vile husks, until at last his cruel hunger drove him, overcome by his long ordeal, to give himself up to the father he had offended and, after confessing his guilt, to seek forgiveness and absolution for his sin. After all that time his kindly father, lifted him up spontaneously from where he lay and with words of comfort gave solace to his son's trembling shame. The finest garment in the house allowed the returned prodigal to be clothed in honor a second time, and a festive crowd celebrated a joyous banquet. For a son, risen as it were from the dead, had returned to his family, and a bright new vision was restored to a father once deprived of his son. But You, almighty Creator of men and things, although You would like all things to remain sound and true, nevertheless suffer no harm from the expense our death incurs, nor, whatever perishes, can any loss diminish Your wealth. You do not know how to grow larger or smaller, and Your glory is constant, Your reign complete. But return to Your servants, Lord, what Adam lost, and whatever the state the roots of our now tainted stock enjoyed in the beginning, may a better life restore it now as we are reborn. Our ancient nature may be soiled and clothed in a cloak torn to shreds, but, Father, take off our torn garment along with our sin and provide the finest cloak for Your returning children. You once had pity on the man found half-dead and forsaken on the road, the man whom thieves had savagely wounded, belabored with blows and stripped of all his clothing. But now, Holy Lord, after having assumed our flesh, You likewise make Your way along a road and, finding a beaten man, do not pass him by. What is more, You carry him, sick as he is, to shelter, using Your own body as a pack horse. We too have sometimes been nothing more than loot in the hands of violent fury, but if grace, which provides oil, and wisdom, which provides wine, now flows over our wounds with a healing balm, and Your right hand entrusts their care to the Samaritans at the inn, then a mighty weakness will be driven from our newly healed bodies. You Who are loath to have the causes of death multiply, listen to the groans which pious hearts pour forth to You in confession. It once happened that a thief hung beside You on that fearful tree, in that time when You were suffering in the flesh, one unlike You in guilt but held fast by the same punishment. With limbs bound but heart free, in spite of the fact that he could not extend a hand pierced by nails, he proclaimed openly what was in his mind and thus, although a criminal paying the penalty he deserved, snatched martyrdom from death. Making a wise end of life, he took the greatest care to make sure that the punishment he was suffering was not wasted. Rather, scaling Heaven's approach, he took it by surprise and, destined as he was to be raised up to Paradise, reached his reward on high with a leap sublime. Extend to us Your heavenly hand, glorious Father, and may life gather us as well to perpetual salvation. Lord, have pity and aid us, who have been deceived by the trick of the great unholy thief, the Devil, as You aided that thief as he suffered with You. May Your even more powerful grace return to their ancient seat those whom the jealous anger of their foe drove from Paradise.

## 4. The Flood

I shall now trace the story of an earth infected by a harmony of sins and of the wickedness that, although legitimized by man, was atoned for by the fatal scourge the flood unleashed. I do not mean the flood in which, the false tale goes, Deucalion scattered over the broad earth stones destined to live in time to come, a hardened race from whom, when they assumed human form, would descend men fit for every labor, who would reveal in their tough minds their stony beginnings. No, since I possess the truth, I shall now take as my subject those waves by means of which a swift destruction, after being unleashed upon things newly created, overtook the fair and fertile earth.

Our mortal race had exalted its haughty spirit in deeds of cruel daring. What each man desired he believed lawful, and his own will assumed the power of law for each individual. Indeed, there was no notion of justice, and so it was thought that there was no distinction between right and wrong, no protection at any time for righteousness, no judge, no witness, not even a guide or arbiter of behavior or one who might urge honesty. Each was his own master when it came to the power of doing injury, and his power came not from good deeds but brute strength. The bolder a man, the better he deemed himself to be. And so, the mind dedicated itself to descending to the ways of beasts and condemned men to lives of bestial behavior. Men grew drunk with blood, and everywhere the flesh of the slain provided torn bits of food for their unrestrained jaws. What is more, they fed on animals who had died a natural death or whom a more ferocious creature had captured and killed, seeing that neither trust nor law restrained them. Indeed, in this, my unsullied song, it is improper to recount how, as if in a herd of animals, unrestrained passion and licentiousness spread in public, as the bonds of morality were broken, how the centers of extravagance and the marketplaces of the foul world seethed with sin.

The wicked race of men, with deeds of this kind and of this enormity, broke nature's contract and took on a crude rustic ferocity, at once abandoning reason and growing wild. The image of their celestial Lord lay forsaken, and because of this foul rejection their minds were deprived of all dignity. In this same way a fertile expanse of beautiful farm land, which the forest yields when it is cut down and cleared of trees, as long as it is cultivated, remains fecund and obedient to man's careful tending. Then it is subject to the hoe and responds with its crops; then the country's beauty preserves itself with a well-ordered appearance. But when, as often happens, the forgetful farmer lets his arms fall at his sides, loosens his grip and enjoys a respite from the weary task of ploughing, then at first the turf grows hard and the earth sluggish. Soon, rough with untended branches and thick shoots, it grows unaccustomed to putting forth cultivated crops. It abounds in worthless shrubs and threatens to become once again a forest. Next, if a woodsman were not to clear it at the last moment with his scythe, it would become a grove, covered not, as now, with bushes but with dense trees; it would push barren leaves into the air until, as its branches ran together, shadows closed over it, and soon, with the sun excluded, the convenient darkness would invite wild animals to trust it as a safe haunt. In the same way the life of the human race, without any true order, after the earliest concepts of law had been lost, tended little by little to take a baser course and fall into depravity. It was ever more steadfast in the very exercise of the sin it fostered with unflagging zeal. And yet, the increasing boldness of each generation's decadent descendants grew even shrewder and more skilled with every lapse into error, as each man surpassed the inventor of his vice and the teacher of his crime.

When at first a stream pours from a small jar, it produces a bright source of water which flows gently and which, at the beginning of its course, everyone can cross with an easy leap. But as soon as it is drawn down from its bubbling spring, it grows with a sudden strength. Then, forcing back its banks, it pushes its rising waters through the plain, occupies the intervening expanse and threatens the farm land with erosion. Next, as it glides along, it swallows up the streams that flow along the neighboring valleys and begins, by its own increase, to mark the end of other rivers, for these are mingled under a single name with the earth that has been eroded by the spreading waters, with timber and the stalls of cattle and dens of wild beasts. Finally, after a long journey, the river gains a fury of its own and grows more violent until it too reaches its terminus at last and is borne into the waters of the sea.

Moving in the same way, the human race advanced like a whirlpool in sin, and strangely the very lengthening of men's lives destroyed their sickened minds. Since life was stubborn and often continued for nine times a hundred years, the long postponement of death removed all terror. And if a tardy fate did carry someone off, he was considered as one who had not been born and had never been, therefore, in danger of being carried off by death. And so, no one cherished a hope for future life, and this world alone planted in their blind senses every kind of fatal passion. At about the same time, even the earth turned sinner and nourished those enormous monsters, the cruel race of giants. We may not, however, tell from what seed they arose. The story used to be told that they all had a common origin and a single mother, but the mystery that surrounds them prevents our telling from what race or what fathers they sprang. If you would ask what they looked like, know only that they had more of a human countenance than a human form. Their features resembled man's and they were like in their limbs, but much different in size. For this reason, Greece, in its works of fiction, later exaggerated their indescribable repulsiveness by giving them shapeless hulks and drawing their bodies with fantastic limbs. In their stories these creatures have the form of men down to their private parts, at which point grafted snakes, as if huge legs, fill out the lower parts of their bodies. Black the snakes are and they equip their half-human limbs with gaping jaws, which, when their heads turn down, provide the giants with the means of locomotion. They also tell that with their blaspheming soles they are accustomed, when terror moves them, to hurl insults at the Thunderer in the sky and that their biting feet roar when the poison in them is stirred. The false story of the Phlegraean war is the same and tells of how these creatures cut out rocks and hurled them through the air, of how a huge hand scattered mountains in a whirlwind as if they were weapons and shook Heaven itself with the pieces of earth it launched.

These are the things the Greek poets in their lying poems tell of the terror bred by primeval giants. But, in the story I tell, every man was rebellious and eager to clash in daring combat, and he who could not join battle with weapons took it up with cruel oaths. It is surely wrong to believe that mountains were ever heaped on mountains, and yet, in time, I shall come to believe that men tried even that, those who thought that they could, with their proud hands, raise on high baked bricks joined with sticky bitumen, who thought that their skyscrapers could reach the stars. In those days the race of mortals went mad and, toiling in vain, piled ineffectual concrete higher and higher, transcending the clouds, pursuing the fleeing sky with their structures, not giving up until discord sent them a sudden multiplicity of languages and their different tongues confounded all.

For this reason, when the laws of language were torn apart, the builders' confused arrogance dashed to bits the criminal compact they had agreed to. Each person joined the group whose words he could understand and each nation adopted a new tongue. And so the top of their abandoned structure was never completed, and the unfinished tower stopped in mid-air. These things happened even after the Flood, for in ancient times how many gigantic citadels did the burdened earth produce and how contemptuous was it in its assault upon the stars. However, since God has purged the world, it is enough to condemn this with our silence. The Creator of man and nature, patient for a long time, kept watching the people of the earth in their mad rage, waiting to see whether a more righteous concern would counsel any of them to leave their association with the empty world and come to their senses. But after the world had decided to run the course of destruction it had sworn to run and set out upon, after it had carried the day and gathered in through all the gates of feeling the ensigns of sin, when no one in his headlong plunge was able to stop and change his path, then the divine Author, viewing the world He had made, shuddered and was filled with grief. Then, in His agitation, they say He thundered threats like these from on high and let loose with His words the anger that had been provoked.

"O barbarous race of men, attracted by nothing that is good and checked by no law, subject only to the ancient snake, more corrupt in each succeeding age! Not enough that Eve fell. No, that inventor of death is now surpassed by each lapse of yours. Nor is it enough that the serpent in ages past overcame Adam in his innocence. Your life, not content with the pollution its parent worked, strives to merit death in its own right. And moreover, I waited this long to no avail, for your sins have stolen all the time I gave you in hope of being able to grant a pardon. Now patience has checked My long-lived anger more than it should have, now is the time for vengeance. This time the flame of Our zeal will not launch thunderbolts from Heaven, nor will the sinking earth, burdened by greater turmoil than it can bear, fall into a vast gulf. Rather, the world, now filthy with sin, will be destroyed by a flood. Let the appearance of the earth rush back to ancient chaos, let mountains of waves return to their former places, let the dry land give way to the water and let formless moisture cover the buried face of the earth again. Be this the death of all living things and the end of the flesh." Thus the eternal Father, dispensing death for all things, shook from His right hand a deluge that fell upon every land.

In the entire world there lived at that time only one just man and he alone had an upright mind. No one beside him bore offerings to God with gifts and prayers. The mighty Creator knew that he deserved praise and, making an exception of him, set about saving him for life. He came from a holy family, for he was noble and descended from a distinguished ancestor, whom old-fashioned faith along with recognized virtue had borne to heaven without death's intervention. A descendent not unlike his forebears in his great deeds succeeded this man and his lofty ideals. Nor is it so great a marvel that the earlier ancestor Enoch left this earthly abode and entered Heaven still able to use the body God had preserved. For in fact it is written that, after a long interval, Elijah followed in his own chariot and, climbing to the place to which old Enoch had once ascended, entered Heaven in his fiery car. His air-borne course traversed the swift winds, and the hooves of his steeds pressed with their weight upon the trodden clouds. The fire that bore the holy man did not scorch him, shielded as he was, and its flame, although it maintained the car's motion, was ignorant of heat. Surely it is remarkable enough that these men were allowed to attain Heaven while still left the use of their bodily limbs. I shall not, however, be any slower to admire the fact that because of his merit Noah alone, that holy man, was able, in his age, to provide salvation for those under his care, his children and their wives, even as the world was destroyed.

There is an angelic chorus in Heaven that surpasses all number and is without end. With perpetual praise its members proclaim and celebrate God, accustomed as they are to giving obedient service and obeying commands from on high. It is they who now receive whatever just prayer mortal hearts make, whatever deserving pleas are formed within a pious breast, whatever a generous hand scatters among the gathered poor. These they bear in hallowed flight beyond the stars. They also watch over the just while their fragile lives exhaust them and keep them safe amid the dangers of the world. Among all the others, however, he is superior in brilliance by whom each of God's greatest works is carried out in the manner of a steward serving his Lord. It is he who prepares God's mysteries in matters of greatest importance. It was he who at God's command announced that the Lord of Heaven would come, assuming a human body in the pure womb of a virgin and it was he who filled that holy womb with the Word as a bridal gift. He also appeared as a messenger before the Baptist's birth, bearing to his father word of the offspring he had long despaired of. He terrified the man as he was making sacrifice and silenced at once the words of doubt upon his ungrateful lips, until at last an aged wife's fertility was manifest in the birth of the child he had predicted. She, who for many years had remained barren, in spite of her despair, felt the pain of labor and bore a child. He, the wise and mighty archangel, enveloped by gentle breezes, set the fluttering wings on his fiery body in motion and with a movement no man could see came from on high through waves of air to earth. It happened that at that moment Noah was weeping for the sins of his fellow men. On the ground, with bent knees and a suppliant's cry, he was begging for the world's creatures a pardon the world itself rejected. When, although the doors were closed, the winged messenger suddenly entered, he appeared as a striking vision surrounded by the light his face emitted. The heroic man was terrified by the overwhelming sight and trembled, for his mortal eye was able only with difficulty to endure the appearance of the heavenly person, and he turned his face and gaze away in fear. But the angel, coming forward to soothe his initial fear with his message of salvation, delivered Heaven's commands: "Peace be to you, just man. I have been sent from Heaven and beseech you to be at peace so that, once your fear is gone, you can listen to my words. The mighty Creator of earth and sea sends you these commands. It is in fact the case that an unexpected sentence of death hangs over all other men. You alone, however, you who deserve to survive, may know this in advance. For your disdain for pleasure has for some time set you apart from the entire world as a righteous man. Now, since your singular life has the power to keep cruel death away from you, I shall outline for you step by step how you should begin to ward off the mighty destruction that is coming. The end of the world will occur when rain is unleashed on every side and the earth is destroyed in the abyss that opens up. Now here is what to do: gather wood and raise up a frame of great strength which will rise and swim above all the waves. It will extend three-hundred cubits in length and in width it should be enclosed by twice five and twice twenty cubits. Its highest point will rise as high as thirty cubits. In the middle of this ship, in a long row, lofty cabins in tiers with overhanging compartments will also rise, and these will enable you, their keeper, to preserve the partners of each living species and arrange separate sleeping spaces for them in the stables you have constructed. Then, to guard against the chance that leaky openings in the joints might let in unwelcome rain, remember to coat the seams of the sides and pour sticky bitumen on them. When you have done everything in this way and made your dwelling complete, go into it at once and abandon the tottering world. Let life begin to close in on those whom continued sin has closed out, and round about you, as you are saved, let their deaths resound. I am going to order you to let your wife come under your roof as well and to let your children enter with their spouses too. You will be the second author of this annihilated race, and, as a result the earth will be replenished with you as sire, in the place of our first author. But because it is not proper, once God's power has finished the world, once His work is done, His law-giving and the consecration of the Sabbath complete, for anything further to be created, to prevent each kind of creature from utterly succumbing to death, take with you two of all the herds of animals that feed upon the air, of the swift birds and wild creatures of the forests, as well as those that are called beasts of burden and those that, creeping, slip along with silent movements. Shut them up with you in the hold of your ship for their survival. Do this in such a way, however, that their restraints keep them with their own mates, for this is the way that the earth must be replenished and renew each race once more. Do not be afraid that the animals will continue in their wild behavior or angrily threaten with their jaws as they generally do. There will be a compact among all whom nature has made quarrelsome in one way or another, and whatever animal you enclose there, trusting and in peace, will obey your commands. At all times, however, beware of the deceits of the serpent alone. With his bent head and the sweet hiss of his triple-forked tongue, he may feign gentle obedience and hide his undying hatred; but never trust him, for he is the creature that Adam, all too wise after his experience, warns you to avoid. Remember: whoever was your enemy once and wished you harm will always be suspect and must be watched with the greatest care, lest he, so clever at lying, even now join in some plot against you. With this example in mind, remember to carry out my commands."

When he had delivered this message, he swept apart the vacant air with his swift wings. Fleeing the vision of man, he was borne aloft and, having delivered God's instructions, left the shaken hero behind. And Noah lifted up his hands and spoke these words: "Whoever you are, either sent by another or come of your own accord from beyond that high crystalline sphere to promise this wondrous salvation and to consecrate with a pledge this treaty gracious and kind, be my patron. Let what you have promised confirm your words and bring your aid to our efforts, so that this puny hand of mine may be strong enough to produce a structure of such magnitude."

With these few words he restored to his heart the hope of life and quickly turned his attention to the instructions he had received on how to carry out his holy labor. What insight, however profound, could grasp, what speech explain how much wood was carried to that place? The hills were stripped, the forests despoiled of their trees. Each mountain, as its nature dictated, did the builder's pleasure, devoting itself obediently to the enterprise. While Pelion sent immense oaks from its peak,

Ossa provided a copse that had been cut down with great effort. The lofty fir was dragged down from Pindus and Atlas, resounding with the sound of chopping, felt the blows of strange axes and gave the ship her knotty pines. And so the invincible fabric began to rise, and its towering penthouse was nailed together and supported by long beams.

As this task was being accomplished, the fickle mob took different sides. Many mocked the man as he made ready his mighty bulwark against the waters, because the hull would never be able to be moved or launched in a river. Even the broad Euphrates, they cried, or Nile would have difficulty accommodating it between their banks. O unbelieving mind of man, why advance the vain opinion that a mortal hand will be unable to join that remote structure with the sea, when the sea will, of its own accord, come to meet it, and the structure, without moving, will touch the shore that draws near? On the other hand, the strangeness of the undertaking drove others, although ignorant of the approaching massacre and the hidden reason for the work, to marvel at and stand in awe of the towering hull with its rugged frame. Their conflicting enthusiasms divided all of them, just as the world's distractions take hold of us now. Today, there are some who dedicate their hearts, once stirred, to faithful service, who know the final peril that closes in on the world, that peril in which all that is corporeal will crumble, in which the centuries will consume all the flesh that has held its revel too long. Then that man will escape the coming evil who has made preparations and built a strong ark of enduring protection. Saved from the waters by the life-giving wood of the cross, he will behold in that moment the great reward for which he held the dissolute life of sin in contempt.

Would not any man, lazy when it comes to making money and fed up with work, think Noah insane as he beheld him nearby intent on his work? Would he not think him insane for being the only one to fret over so foolish a worry, for refusing to profit from a world in decline? This is the way the glutton mocks the abstemious man, the way the miser mocks the generous, the thief his victim and the adulterer the chaste. This is the way the swindler rejoices in making the simple man look ridiculous and the way the rich man, as he collects his gold, laments the folly of one who distributes his wealth and who, poor by his own choice, uses up his riches and becomes wretched in material things but prosperous in hope.

There will come a time sudden and unlooked for, when the eternal Judge will see that doomsday is approaching, and He will say, "The end threatens with the same swiftness as it did ages ago in the time of Noah, the Just, when the flood discovered all the different things men had done and consumed all flesh with its waters, when the builder of salvation escaped the all-engulfing danger in the fortress he had made." These things have been proclaimed in the parables of the gospels.

In the meantime, knowing as he did what was going to happen, the builder completed the ark. Then, at his command, the winged birds flocked to it; every beast left its accustomed haunt under the forest's roof and, its ferocity put aside, came to meet him. Each eagerly embraced its own captivity and even rejoiced in imprisonment when its freedom was gone. To such an extent does the hidden power of what is to come prevail. A concealed terror burned in the animals' senses, and their being grew restless with anticipatory fear. But mankind, which a certain doom was pursuing, remained unafraid even with death so close. It is our general belief that fear often gives an early life-giving warning of coming death, but until the very moment of their destruction, the sentence of death found the guilty inhabitants of Gomorrah carefree and happy. For the people of Nineveh, however, in the place of tranquility, fear, accompanied by healing terror, prevailed. For to that place the prophet had come as bidden. Much buffeted on land and sea, he who would proclaim that mighty people's destruction feared a flood, although he realized that the world would remain secure. The whale had swum toward him when he was in the sea and had swallowed him with its mighty jaws, closing him up in the ark of its stomach. Now the power may have been given to that raging monster to swallow up the man and fill its ample jaws, but it was not permitted to chew him up, and so the prophet was untouched by the beast's teeth. That counterfeit prey entered the voracious beast and, having entered, lived there as if food within the hungry belly. Finally, when the sun had measured in light a journey of three days, a journey that equalled the prophet's one night, the whale-prison, wanting to be free of its captive, saw a strange shore and vomited its punished meal upon it.

When the seer had been set free from the monster, when he saw the sky and touched the earth, he made for the great city in his excitement, calling out a frightening message. "Why," he cried, "are you afire with the flames of sin? Your punishment is going to extinguish all, for the end is now approaching. My warning has come late but still it has come." He said no more, but all the people came together and made every kind of lamentation. On all sides their tears gushed forth. Breasts were beaten and sighs struck the sky. They cast aside their soft coverlets and wrapped themselves in rough shaggy blankets. They poured ashes into their food and tears into their drink. And their king, a worthy leader in an hour like that, carried the standard of salvation before their weeping line and, strange to tell, in his fear he overcame the threatening danger. He cast away his sceptre, left his lofty tribunal, and, scorning its golden clasp, contemptuously unfastened his robe of purple and donned a rough cloak.

In those days, however, the world's righteous Lord, surveying such events from Heaven, checked the wrath He had revealed, stayed his hand and, holding his poised weapon still, extinguished its bolt. It was to be the same for that just man, the ark's builder, when in his own age he would rejoice in having been the only one to fear destruction in an otherwise carefree world, rejoice in perceiving that the fates of men, which vary in accordance with the merits of each, would bring death to everyone else, salvation to him. And so when he had gathered and caged the wild beasts of either sex, he chose for the voyage cattle that were called clean and might be eaten. From these he consigned to his fortress just seven of each creature so that, saving their seed by saving three pairs, he might at some time offer the seventh ones in sacrifice. Now the life-giving prison held everything inside it, and its open hatches received the just builder himself along with all of his children and their mates, placing them in safe-keeping for the life that was to come. Remember, that at that time nature had not yet given to some the name of slave, nor did the order of things know the distinction between master and servant. It was in fact Noah's middle son who first knew the disgrace of a servile name. By chance and in jest the poor boy tried to catch sight of his father naked and, although more unsightly himself, this son laughed at his own maker. Then the fool appeared even baser when his simple-mindedness was exposed. For when holy Noah learned of what the boy had done, he gave him to his brothers as a slave. That is how that yoke came into being, for we are all born of one seed. An individual's guilt is surely revealed as the cause of slavery. Just so, a free man, when he sins, becomes a slave to his crime, but if an upright man is confined in servitude he creates his own circumstances of birth and becomes noble.

Now the messenger who had lately been sent to bring the gift of Heaven's word to the just hero, quickly descended once again from Heaven as soon as he saw Noah enclosed in the ark, ready and waiting for the appointed day. He fixed the loose hatches with hinges, closed the passengers inside and dragged the sturdy portals shut. Then, rising quickly, he returned to Heaven. This happened at a time when old Noah was six hundred years old and when the month-making moon had twice added a full cycle to his next year. The seventeenth day after these two months would dawn for the world as its last and even in that moment consign everything to death.

Then, all at once, heaven was covered by a great darkness, and the light of the dusky sun faded and was blotted out. Scarcely had terror begun to touch the crazed minds of men when an unusual cloud drifted down from the sky. Looking at first like a mighty storm, it was unleashed upon them. All of the earth's continents from one end of the world to the other grew wet at the same moment, and the entire sky took on a single cloudy appearance. Then Egypt itself trembled before these strange waters, the inundated Garamantidian grew cold, and the wet chill penetrated even the Massylian Syrtes, whose climate had long been warm. Not for long, however, did the storm retain the appearance of rain, nor in the end did mere drops fall. Rather, heaven burst open and rivers poured down. In the same way the Tanais, when it is fed with snow, rushes like a white torrent from the Riphaean mountains and dashes along its course, and whatever it brings down its long path it hurls headlong downstream as it goes. This was the kind of contest of breakers that shook the earth, as the air, hedged in by waves, put up a fight. It was not, however, the sky alone that rained water, for the earth too rose up in terrestrial anger. All the soil was cleft and the fields yielded many wandering streams. Fountains leapt up and rivers hitherto unknown began to flow. Clouds, their weight shifted, turned skyward, waves, falling from heaven and springing up everywhere on earth, soon met and, with their fury linked, the elements conspired in the slaughter. All the riverbanks were topped by waves, and the watery torrent, all its restraints now loosened, raged over its broken barriers. Now, even as everything was struggling to engulf the expanse of the wide world and to fill the spacious earth, the sentence of death might perhaps have been held off and postponed by further delay, in which case the final doom might have yielded a brief respite and consumed all creatures of the flesh somewhat later. But the ocean, now a seething whirlpool of elements, burst through that single strand that alone girds land and sea and, breaking its trust, utterly inundated the dry land. It shattered the eternal laws and, leaving its own place, made for strange realms as it threw nature's covenants into confusion.

Then, for the first time, famous rivers felt the ominous raging of the sea, rivers that rumor, itself renowned for its swiftness, makes great in its reports. For a little while the rivers stood amazed at these strange movements, but then you would have thought that they had consciously chosen to flee, given the way they turned back and spread over the earth the billows which the sea had swelled. Next the ocean itself followed, threatening the retreating streams and driving the rivers back with great salty masses of water. With the onset of this mighty roar an even greater fear struck men in their grief. They climbed towers and the high roofs of their houses and rejoiced in postponing even for a little while the death that faced them. The rising water dragged many away as they tried to climb. Some it pursued as they made for the mountains and snatched away their empty flight by killing them. Others, limbs thrashing in an endless swim, tired at last and gave up the ghost. Still other bodies, giving up their lives on whatever mountain they could reach, were overcome by the clouds' heavy burden and imbibed the streaming waters that sea and rivers had mixed together. Buildings were knocked down, and other men perished in their fall, as house and master plunged together into the waves. A roar made up of every kind of sound rose to Heaven, and amid the human carnage the herds of falling animals added to the confused tumult by mingling their cries with those of men. As this universal death seethed up over the sad earth, the recently loaded ark was struck by a wild movement. Its structure trembled and its groaning joints strained. The unholy power of the flood did not, however, penetrate its hull, even though it lashed and weakened the solid ship with its beating waves.

In the same way the true Church endures many storms and even now is troubled by violent waves. On one side the uncouth pagan rouses his swollen fury, on the other Judaea rages and raises against it its raving voice. On yet another side, in a frenzy, the wild Charybdis of heresy provokes it, and the pompous wisdom of the Greek philosophers is happy to commit itself to the struggle among the swelling waves. False claims stir empty winds with their slander but beat in vain against the bulwark of the Church with their empty roar.

But now the rising waves had covered the middle of the ark and, supporting it on every side, moved the hull, which was safer because of the natural buoyancy that lifted it. Wherever the waves called, the weighty mass, now mobile, followed. We too should yield to the world in this way as long as we are subject to it. For whatever resists utterly and knows not how to bend, must be afraid of snapping under pressure. Rather, let us yield as the ark did, lest our impervious minds experience an inward weakening and draw in some sin. Now all this time that fountain of life, entrusted as it was to the wandering bark, sailed on, and the sea itself, as it raged over all of creation, preserved him as the earth's treasure. So too would it render that treasure up again as a faithful guardian should when the earthly peace that had been promised demanded its return.

And so the waves came and all of the earth was submerged. The waters flowed over the hills and overcame even their peaks. Then Othrys, rich in pines, withdrew from view, covered by the sea. The peak of Parnassus exposed not a single lofty crag, and even the stones of cypress-bearing Lycaeus lay hidden, as were the Alps, now nothing more than submerged rocks sunken deep beneath the waves. Everything was gone and in the end the whole world was sky and sea. Since all other creatures had been destroyed by death, the monsters of the ocean reigned in the wooded whirlpool, and the watery sea beat against the adjacent sky. For forty nights the storm poured down and accomplished its slaughter. Death no longer had anything to destroy, for the sea submerged the floating corpses too. Then at last the rains were checked. The crystalline vault of heaven shone forth and a pleasing aspect returned to the sky. The sun itself returned but found no land to which it might restore its light. It illuminated water alone, and its sad glow looked only upon the sea. Of course, to the extent that its rays were shortened and broke upon the moving waves, to that extent it burned and pressed closer upon the water it had to consume. The openings in the gaping earth closed as well, and the abyss sucked up again the streams which it had earlier spewed from its deadly jaws and confined them within their own banks. But the waters did not recede as quickly as they had come. What a few days had rained down not a few months but a long period of time dried up. And the ark, sailing on, drew close to the tall mountains of Armenia and settled to the bottom on fields not yet exposed.

When the old man realized that the boat had come to rest and was no longer sailing over the windy sea, he imagined that the waters had receded and that the bright earth had reappeared. He opened the topmost window high on the front of the ark to send out a bird to explore the receding waters. The bird flew out, lashing the air with a ceaseless flapping of its wings, which beat at the empty winds as they moved. When, however, he had soared above the waves for a long time and when his wings had grown weary and no place had presented the resting place he was looking for, the bird returned from his scanning of the sea to the familiar boat. The old man clutched him in his hands and brought him inside, noting that no land had yet appeared amid the waters.

Meanwhile the sea, by gathering itself into a single great mass, left the land and was returning to its ancient and chaotic basin. Then at last the peaks of lofty mountains began to come into view for the first time and, after they appeared, the sight of lower hills became more frequent. But when its shores confined the sea as of old, when the hallowed ocean, gathered within its well known bounds and content in its containment, absorbed the rivers which now flowed in their accustomed courses, when it reined in all their streams and when, on all sides, their own channels enclosed these torrents, then, with the water withdrawn, the newly freed earth shone forth. After some time had passed, the old man brought out a raven, for he wanted to examine the empty earth and learn more about it. When the bird stretched its wings and made for the shining air, it looked down at the earth which was now filled with heaps of dead and, settling on this flesh, soon forgot about going back and abandoned his patient master in their common home. Jew, this is like your ignorance of how to keep faith with your Lord. Although freed by Him, you too love the flesh in this way and render no thanks to the Protector and Lord of your life. In the same way, weak and distracted, you wander off; in the same way you have broken the covenant of the law and violated perfidiously its agreement. Now when the old man judged from the length of his wait that the worthless crow had had sufficient time to return to the ark, and since he did not know why it was late in returning or what the cause of its delay was, whether weary and with drooping wings it had succumbed to fate or whether the receding waves had added it to the multitude of rotting dead, he at once sent forth from the ark a white dove. The dove, mindful of his commands, flew swiftly to the dry fields and, seeing the branch of a blossoming olive tree, a symbol of peace, plucked it and brought it to the boat in its gentle beak. With this sign the simple messenger confirmed God's pact, and the holy man discovered the newly purified world.

Its perfect circle kept wheeling the measured year around, and throughout it the happy boat held all those living creatures in its hull. Then in time, father Noah opened the closed hatches by drawing back their bars. He began to restore the unaccustomed sunlight to those within so that their seed might return to the exhausted world. But before the just man ordered them to wander off and scatter themselves over the land, he took one of the seven of each kind of clean animal he had been careful to enclose earlier and, calling his children and their mates, he placed the animals on an altar built of turf and sacrificed them, after lighting holy flames on the altar for the first time. As a great number of bodies were burnt on the huge fire and numerous victims sent up a fatty smoke, a pleasant odor crossed the bright air and touched the joyous sky. The first sacrifices of the cleansed earth were accepted, and then God's voice mingled with the sound of the sacred fire and thundered: "Let the infected earth's pollution extend this far and no further. Let it be sufficient that evil once held sway. Let the earth, cleansed with a washing that is eternal, shine forth, and let the elements keep their restored appearances. Let the mass of the earth no longer lie exposed to evil in its confusion. And you as well, whom life has saved from the hour of death, keeping you safe and defending you against all peril, observe My laws and lead a carefree life. You, the source of this race, with fruitful seed scatter your offspring until they fill the broad earth far and wide. Let them restore the population that was wiped out and rule the earth. What is more, let the animals restore as well their fertile stock, stock that, according to the ancient plan, will bend to your will and serve you. Moreover, on earth from this time forth there will never be another flood so powerful that it wipes out all flesh. That this one was unique a single sign shall signify, and even repeated sins will see no similar slaughter. If there is sin, however, another kind of terror will not be lacking." Thus the heavenly Father sanctified this one baptism, and swore that although the earth had once been washed with cleansing waters, the guilty could no longer hope for a second washing of that kind.

The sun had just traversed three-quarters of the sky, and its oblique beams were inclining toward its setting, when it happened that they were ordered to touch a far-off cloud that lay beneath the eastern sky, and as they did, they caused a sign to leap out of the moisture-laden air. Yes, that arc which poets in the language of the Greeks call Thaumantis and those who write in Romulus' tongue call Iris flashed out. For when the pendent moisture felt the sun passing through it, it sent forth wavering colors that shone with various hues and were beyond counting. Shimmering circles, differing in appearance, played across the apparition as the light filtered through it, one bright sapphire, one dappled, another blue, another white. It drew purple from the cloud, a golden glitter from the sun, brightness from Heaven and darkness from the earth. Now what was made of these separate elements, you would have considered diverse but harmoniously diverse. God produced the lovely shape of the rainbow as a sign for frightened mankind, displaying a sky clear of clouds and promising that no further peril lay in wait for the earth.

Now whichever of you wishes to store up real salvation, you will look to that sign which other signs represent figuratively; for Christ, the Giver of life, sent ahead signs like these, and indeed a similar conjunction of opposite natures gave us a Savior. Within the flesh He assumed on earth within the womb of a shining virgin inheres the brilliance natural to His Father's seed. This Mediator in Heaven on high, a Being in between, as various in the many different gifts He gives, but shining for all, shows us the life-giving arc of His hallowed pledge. See it in your heart, you who are cleansed by baptism, and go to heaven freed of a guilt that has vanished. You may read this in the apostle, who says, "A washing like that which occurred in antiquity, when Noah chose eight souls and enclosed them in the ark, will save you." Christ prepared the gift; it is your duty to cherish and keep it, lodging it in your vows and prayers, seeking this with your tears: that your sins do not return, that what has been drowned does not come to the surface again, that dead things do not rise and things that have been defeated do not raise up a new rebellion, that after your guilt has been washed away spiritual perils do not regain their strength, that you need not fear the flames, in that place where water is not available now.

## 5. The Crossing of the Red Sea

To a poet who has until now been writing about the extent of the waves' power over the land the next chapter of his narrative now reveals land between waves. In the story I have just told, the flood took the initiative and pursued those it destroyed. Now thousands of men on the brink of death, their hearts aflame and brimming with frenzy, will run toward the flood of their own accord. I do not write this to achieve in the narration of so great an event the grace of style it deserves; the desire to render praise to God is enough, along with the hope that this faithful servant's work makes clear my fervent prayer. And surely if someone cannot give thanks in words, he has no small virtue in simply believing in the deeds the ancients have handed down as signs through chosen authors. Among these that story is by far the most remarkable in which that renowned collection of scriptures tells what happened in the Red Sea. In the light of its holy authority, this story represented, more than anything, a pledge of things to come, and the nature of the salvation it promised surpassed in beauty the beauty of the narrative. The work's beauty was great enough at the level of the story it told but still greater in the figurative sense, for within its fecund shell it conceived and brought forth life itself.

God's oppressed people had long endured hard work in a foreign land, serving the Egyptians as subjects. The length of their day's toil galled them, crushing them as it did beneath a burden of thick filth and countless loads of bricks. And they were stung as well by the deceit of a cruel tyrant. For his part he gnashed his teeth at the sight of the hated throng's increase and grieved to see the number of his slaves grow greater. He had in fact given an order that whenever daylight fell upon a newborn male, its midwife should at once slay it and thus shrewdly eliminate that sex at birth; but the women were appalled by this and fled from such acts, refusing to destroy the forbidden offspring. So firmly did God stand by His promise to extend that holy nation's power. And to the extent that the king's blind mind conceived even crueller designs, the seeds of the young nation flourished even more.

Now the Creator, His countenance serene, had been watching these suffering people from His heavenly seat. The holy bush had just produced harmless flames from its kindling, remaining green even as its branches grew red hot. By this sign, we should note, the faith that warms the hearts of the holy may understand that the thorns of our minds burn bright, and yet cast light from a fire that does not consume the pious man. Now after that miracle, the chosen priests at once began to carry out God's commands, as Moses, their leader, addressed these words to the king: "The time has come to free a people weary with the burden of long servitude, to free shoulders oppressed by their heavy loads, necks worn out and hands which continual labor has made hard. Send away those who ask to fulfil at long last their vows to their divine Lord and to perform the rituals the teaching of their ancestors prescribes."

The king replied in a rage: "What is the cause of this wide-spread rebellion? What strange God sends omens and makes demands on these people? Am I to suppose that these empty grievances reach Heaven itself and that the Lord now wants to take slaves of long standing from their masters, that for this reason He sends commands to these haughty rebels? Who can this God be Whom I must obey? What can stir fear in a king who is supreme in his rule? No, too much idleness seduces your minds and, if the rest I grant you did not encourage your laziness, your time would not be wasted on these useless words. If the burden of heavier toil were to correct this tendency and hold it in check, your lawless daring would stop attempting what is forbidden. And you, the ring-leaders who draw up such requests and who, with your empty cries, turned this people against us, avoid my sight and beware of my countenance.

For I call as witness rich Pharon and your streams, all-powerful Nile, and Anubis of voice divine when he howls in fury, it will not go unpunished, if these words make their way back again to our tribunal."

Now it happened that Moses, the patriarch and lawgiver, was holding a staff in his hand, for with this stick to lean upon his right hand would guide his steps. This he hurled a short distance and let it strike the ground with a heavy blow. Then, wonderful to tell, the stick began to wriggle but not in the way it might when life puts forth insensible branches from a stalk, producing only the fruit which it causes to grow. In the end, the staff, creeping along with a twisting motion, possessing both the sensation and life suited to its changed body, began to flee and, before long, it assumed the form of a snake. The tyrant sat still, transfixed by terror and, although he had always been black, turned pale. However, so that his attendant, who stood with head bent beside him, would not see him confused and overwhelmed by such a portent, he pretended that he did not believe that the deed had been accomplished at God's command. Wishing it to be considered not a divine but a human act, he gave instructions to his minister to use vague threats of death to make whatever magicians and chanters of spells, whatever dabblers in illicit arts and dark deceit the great expanse of Egypt could provide, display similar portents. At this command, they assembled from every corner of the land and each armed himself with the wand his own familiar demon had enchanted. When they were thrown down, the wands gave the illusion of snakes which, although imaginary, took in and terrified the eyes of the onlookers with their deceptive appearance. The magicians, however, did not swell with pride for long. Everything they thought they had accomplished was quickly devoured, for the first snake, still eager to unleash its fangs, swallowed with its viper's mouth those that had been formed by the magicians' art. Then, after Moses put an end to this show of power by taking hold of the victor by the tail and lifting it from the ground, the snake departed from the stick and its appearance vanished. As its body grew hard, its wandering coils stiffened. Need I say more? It became the staff it had been and with it the holy man made more portents appear as time passed.

Then the Pharaoh recognized the truth, grew vehement and gnashed his teeth bitterly. As he began to resist the hand of God in everything, he refused to confess what he knew to be so and ordered the two priests Moses and Aaron to be driven from his sight at once. But they assaulted the ears of the Lord with their wailing, praying that at long last God restrain the raging of that evil nation, which divine warnings had only

made more oppressively cruel, had in fact caused to threaten war against
Heaven itself. God the Father took up their groans and tears as they
prayed and gave solace to their bitter hearts with this gentle encourage-
ment: "Do not make your hearts slave to such an empty fear, My peo-
ple, you whom I chose to adopt from the entire population of the earth
and alone, with a destiny all your own, consecrated to Myself. Now you
will see what great aid I shall provide, pressing to a conclusion what you
have begun and pressing in on your cruel enemies as well. I shall turn
My sublime right hand to the production of every conceivable portent,
for the King of Egypt will refuse to yield to a few signs, and My mira-
cles will subdue his stubborn mind only after a long interval. But when
these are accomplished, he will free you, even force you to depart and
drive you from his land. What he now refuses he will freely lavish upon
you. After brave campaigns, you will go to a great homeland where the
rich and fertile earth that awaits you beckons and, after defeating the
neighboring peoples, you will build famous cities there. Only trust in
the gifts I promise, let a strength nourished by joy support the labors
which these mighty works will demand and let it save itself for better
things to come." When they had heard these things, they were seized by
a more powerful hope. Their spirits revived and they extended their
hands to the stars. Faith was conceived within them as they prayed and
they gave thanks to God.

Now tomorrow's light had just given the first faint sign that the sun
was rising, and dawn, as night was swept away, advanced to usher in the
next day. At that hour blood stained the rivers and made the fields wet
with sudden gore. Nor did this portent touch only the lesser streams,
for the Nile, king of rivers itself, grew red and did not reflect with its
former light that special splendor it imbibes at its source. No, its current
was reversed to keep it from reaching its ancient course, and blood
struggled to flow along its furthermost channel, blood that, although an-
imal in appearance, was not of the flesh and did not gush from a body.
Nor could slaughter, however widespread, along with whatever wounds,
have made up for the loss of water with the blood it produced. Then the
displaced fish, their nostrils clogged, were impeded as they struggled to
swim and sinking, perished in the thick eddies, thus adding to the foul
ooze with their own dead bodies. Then, had this itself not been a
punishment, I would perhaps surmise from the bloody evidence that the
catastrophe of carnage and death to come had already taken place, for
the entire expanse of Egypt, even to that place where Canopus opens
into a broad stream, would surely have lain exhausted by thirst amid

those clotted waters, had not the Almighty scattered a quick cure upon those fields and summoned the bright streams back to their beds.

When this plague was withdrawn and peace returned, the tyrant, although his death had been postponed, lost control of himself again and, with little thought for the punishment he had barely avoided, he stubbornly continued to subject the innocent nation to the whip. But why should my pen seethe in order to tell the whole tale of that arrogant monarch's perfidy, enumerating the false promises of that doomed realm? And yet, their mendacity did in fact elicit other portents. Scarcely had the waves been cleansed of the gore that lapped at the river banks, when they covered the cities with the ugly croaking of frogs. Rooms were filled with them, along with beds, inner chambers and tables. Even he who wore the royal purple had to put up with their endless leaping and, even as he was oppressing men, grew livid at having to yield to frogs. But soon, with a stroke of thunder, the horde of frogs was killed, only to be replaced by a buzzing swarm of flies that burst into the sky from the heaps of dead frogs, corrupting the breezes with infected air. And just as many flights of the insects called gnats committed their suspended bodies to the light winds there and fluttered up and down on buzzing wings. Together these swarmed out to fill the confused city, and although they inflicted wounds with bites that punctured the skin, fear of them agitated men more than the actual punishment they inflicted. But a driving wind swept them away too, and the plague on Egypt was relaxed and receded a little. At once the king's fear left him and he felt God's wrath no longer than the heat of His scourge. And yet, even when that plague had been withdrawn others followed with still deadlier effect. All the cattle were consumed by the next, as a single night witnessed the destruction of the nation's entire flock. But not even these portentous events, destructive as they were, wore the guilty Egyptians down. And so an anger that would initiate new sufferings now turned against their own flesh. Swelling boils grew deep in their limbs, and a cursed fire settled in their stricken joints. Even this weakness, however, they believed had overtaken them by chance, while, in fact, the disease of their minds was causing the bodily peril. That day passed and then, at last, on the following morning, the sky was struck with thunder and the gathering clouds flashed with a terrible splendor. A brilliance gathered itself into a bolt of lightning and struck everything in sight as, beneath the turmoil of the sky, the elements threatened the earth with total and instantaneous destruction. Hail of great weight was mixed with fire and fell to earth, not in a storm cloud as is normal, but in chunks capable of crushing and bringing destruction to each victim with their impact alone. The iciness of the hail was then joined in the air with seething flames, and nature, preserving the power of both, made them instruments for meting out death. At first the storm produced its carnage by killing in a random way, but then, to consume the remaining crops, the Brucus swept in, the locust that trusts in the power of its extended legs. But even then the king's unfeeling pride, schooled first by evil, now by one disaster after another, continued to consider these things easy to endure. However, divine anger, ever swift, brought on an even deadlier vindication. On the next morning the rising sun had scattered the dark shadows and was shining joyfully as it turned toward the earth a countenance filled with tranquil light, when suddenly a black cloud arose and extended itself across the middle of the sky, driving the light away and shutting out the day that was dawning. A thick night gathered itself into a mass. The air was smothered and succumbed. Men's groping hands could feel the thick darkness, and their painful breathing was shaken and troubled. If anyone had a mind to rouse smoldering fires by blowing upon them or wanted to stir their flames, the fire's light was extinguished and died. Nor did it unfurl tongues of fire, muffled as these were by the weight of the foul atmosphere. Wherever the black horror found a man, it held him fast, for he saw no one and was seen by none. You would have thought that a thousand creatures had entered the murky halls of the dead together or that by chance the barrier of the earth's surface had been pulled away, that the land of the foul abyss had shifted to the realms above it and that, with light gone, had subjected the world to its own laws. During that night the earth paid the penalty for those whose perjury deserved it, and lost three days. That was something the condemned alone experienced, however, for the bright orb above held everything else within its circuit and time continued to mark its normal course.

In the meantime, Moses was steadfast, weeping, fasting and making promises to God. With prayer after prayer he carried out his vigil, supported by the solace his elder brother gave. And the Creator instructed them in holy observances, teaching them so that a mystic victim might reveal a sacred rite. "You see," He said, "how Egypt struggles under this great catastrophe, how, afflicted on every side, it is worn down, and pays in lamentation what its guilt requires. And yet, the rebel remains stiff-necked and stubborn. These events, beyond long endurance, are merely a prelude to his downfall. Whatever swells up as he does is sick, for there is nothing sound in a haughty man, and his swollen mind shows that death clings to him. One more agony, which will vindicate all, remains. After nine have been tried in vain, let it cut down those who deserve it in a tenth harvest of death. As for you, your only task is to learn rituals that will survive forever and to abide by your own observances under an enduring law. Among all the months which the year's orbit circumscribes, that shall be first and foremost, which the Gentiles call by the name of War, but which you are to call simply the First. In that month when the moon has added fourteen nights to its course, then, late in the evening, you will begin your rites. Take a gentle lamb of just the right age, a lamb without stain, whose body has a spotless fleece. This animal you will slaughter for your feast day, and the blood of its bright body will mark both of your doorposts. It is concern for your safety that will make this mark. When the killer comes and without bloodshed accomplishes his silent slaughter, make sure that he sees that your door is wet with the holy blood, for only such a one will he be willing to pass by, and that distinction will protect your house from the death he will mete out." As Your sign, Christ, when it is placed on our foreheads, is our best salvation, so let the holy blood shed by the pre-ordained Lamb and poured into our mouths now, be believed to have cleansed the portals of Your people, even as the tottering world seethed with dying and as the blade touched with death those unmarked; and let that same blood keep Your people from every misfortune. Understand, reader, the special meaning and significance of this for you, living as you do among a people marked for salvation. Henceforth in whatever place the gentle Lamb is sacrificed and the Victim provides its holy body as food, let those who abide by His promises of life fittingly perform their own holy ceremony. Plucking from their false hearts a yeast without value, let them sprinkle around them the true leaven of a radiant mind.

The divine Teacher had finished giving the laws and covenants of the paschal holiday to the men of the nation, and they all accepted them at once. They were happy to hold those banquets and to set out, in this new act of worship, the ceremonial food. It was a ritual that, once established, would be passed down to their descendants in ages to come. Night had come and, since the darkness had just marked the division between its two halves, all creatures were enjoying the hush of its middle hours. And behold, with quiet tread, the angel came through the ominous silence, he who had been sent by God to wreak havoc with his drawn blade. Nor was it to be some universal sentence of instantaneous death that would be handed down. On the contrary, every evil fell to its victim by design and each one whom the course of pre-ordained death would seek out in the darkness was doomed long before. The eldest sons were the ones who perished, for they alone were chosen for death whom birth had presented to the light first. Young servants perished with their masters, and the sons of the powerful fell along with commoners. The poor young man died and so did he whom the purple of a tall bedstead propped up in death with its proud support. Bodies were strewn in death on unlike beds, some naked on the earth, others wrapped in silk. Impartial death feared no one and made no exceptions for any honors, things noted among the living only; for death remains unmoved by human feeling even when a pauper weeps, nor can it be bribed by gold to spare the rich. The healthy son made his journey before the ill, the young before the old. No man, you see, should place his trust in health or age alone. There is, however, one way alone in which the dead differ among themselves, in that they who fill out their allotted span of life may live on because of their good deeds. Here death never has absolute rights, although it may use its own power to carry off what is made of earthly parts, what is born of human seed and what is returned to earth. From the deeds of the just, however, nothing is ceded to death, in whatever form it comes.

Then when the royal court, in sudden confusion, saw its sons stricken, the mothers of the youths ran weeping to their dead bodies. Death was spread open to view on every side, and yet the cause of death in the form of wounds did not appear. The Egyptians struck their breasts with their fists, tore their hair and instinctively clawed at their black cheeks with their nails. Nor did those watching weep long for their lords alone, for before long each experienced his own grief. A single cry struck the sky but arose not from a single weeping, and no house that lent its voice to the uproar was free of death. Next, with many a light, countless funerals were performed throughout the city, and the declaration of a proper period of mourning moved the guilty nation to display its grief. In that hour, even as each prolonged his own grief and lamentation, sorrow itself postponed the rites of the dead, and for a time the unburied multitude lay scattered here and there deprived of burial. And so they would have continued to lie, had not a band, gathered with difficulty to commit the many dead to urns, either placed the exposed and unhonored corpses in the barren earth at long last or cremated them on a funeral pyre.

A sad throng stood around the king and began to mutter to themselves, voicing their humble complaints. "Alas, too great is the power

turned against our state by the Hebrew people, for whom every evil
again and again takes up arms with a vengeful hand, for whom the
whole world finally fights, for whom only blessings descend from the
otherwise angry sky. Some secret power of God, some greater force
rages against this kingdom and avenges that nation at the cost of the rest
of the world. The elements, as they decay, preserve these victorious peo-
ple as if they were their own and redeem them with their own collapse.
See how Egypt now lies broken beyond repair. If only the hand of God
would bring, as it has until now, punishment to the living alone and loss
to our fields. Would that it had not killed so many and then cheated and
emptied Canopus with this sudden bloodbath. Now, at long last, have
mercy on this land and drive out those who cause our ruin, even now
while the slaughter is still moderate, while some still look upon the sun-
light, still survive to press them from behind, to drive them from our
border, not to suffer them to remain if by chance they should, in their
craven hearts, wish to linger here. No, banish this bloodshed by ejecting
these foreigners. Let our grief for our dead sons move you. Let, perhaps,
your own grief move you. A few children may still remain, and these,
if saved, may have the power to wash away our great grief and repair
the loss to our maimed nation." The people added their tears to these
words, and the haughty monarch lost his composure as they wept and
confessed that he was beaten.

   While this crisis in the king's troubled court was being dealt with,
the Hebrews, in accordance with their priests' wishes and with God's in-
structions, pretended that they needed all the Egyptians' finest posses-
sions for sacred rites and banquets, and asked them to give them the ves-
sels which their ceremonial worship would demand in great number
along with ornaments and garments, jewelry and gems. Nor were their
hosts slow to supply these things. Indeed, an ignorant band of Egyptians
vied with one another in making the frightened nation rich. Almighty
Father, You who treated so cruel an enemy in this way, what mouths
are worthy to be opened in Your praise? Yes, their foe acquiesced and
in spite of himself lavished gifts on them, which they would carry with
them as they were set free. For You considered it not sufficient simply
to free the oppressed, but You made them rich as they went, and their
restored freedom took possession of new treasures. Living in a hostile
land, with violence raging all around them, the fugitives despoiled their
master, deceiving him as he watched, and stripped his house in his pres-
ence. You would have imagined not that they were being driven to de-
part but that they were joyfully moving to a new land. And so the

riches of the greedy Pharaoh were carried off and, seeing them, you might well have come to the conclusion that he was paying the price that had been assessed for their slavery's long toil. Sometimes what seems misfortune works to the advantage of the just, and what an evil man wishes to be a curse is changed by God's influence into a blessing. The destructive power of hatred draws the guilty alone toward the very wound they planned for others and drives them into the noose they prepared for their brothers.

Now the royal ministers left their frightened king and, driving the Hebrews forward, forced them, willing as they were to go, to be even quicker in their flight. They swooped down, pressed swiftly upon them even as they hurried along, for they believed that their own destruction would be driven away with the expulsion of that hated nation. The foreigners had now completed nearly five hundred years in your kingdom, Egypt, from that early time when Jacob, the ancient patriarch, had brought his household there with his twelve sons and their beloved descendants; and from that fertile stock a multitude had grown. Now at last the people were departing and before long, with ranks closed, they left the dread land, childless, in darkness and grief. The next day had not yet dawned, and it would be the night that would free them from their enemy and that would be established as a holiday for the people, an annual celebration on which their holy sacrifices to God would be renewed.

In clear view in the first rank, their commander and lawgiver was radiant as he led their column with his brother at his side. Behind them the line of warriors fell into battle order and marched in front of the troops of horse, mighty in their own strong formations. They bore their arms on their shoulders, and their blades hung from their belts on the left side. Their heads were helmeted and blazed with a metallic glow that challenged the white light of the moon. Others leaned on javelins or spun shields in their left hands, thinking on war as the shields ran swiftly round and round. Another unit took joy in its quivers and fit into them winged arrows for dispatching death against the attacking enemy or for sending winged shafts on the light wind whenever they happened to be pursuing the backs of a fleeing foe.

The frightened common folk marched in the last ranks. In number they were like the stars with which the sky is decorated, or the motion of the sea as it foams with cresting waves. They were as many as the sands which the breakers sweep upon the shore or as numerous as the drops which water-laden clouds rain down. The generals of the Pharaoh stood in wonder and realized that they could never have conceived of the throng's magnitude. What is more, they were pleased to have driven out so many foemen. And yet, the edge of your battleline was not to be saved by a blade's edge, Hebrew warriors, even though you made it dense with countless companies of soldiers. No, their Author alone would fight on behalf of all those thousands of men. Now, however, the people, slowly beginning their long and tedious journey, were making their way along the course they had set out on. Their leaders deliberately advanced at a pace that slow old age and creeping infancy, its years still tender, could bear, this lest an untimely effort for which they were not ready bring grief to those weak in age or sex as they went. And so, God's will arranged everything, and He took His place beside His rejoicing people.

Then, when the multitude had settled within their fortified camp and the infantry had encircled the unarmed common folk, as evening fell, a flame in the form of an upright column presented itself to them and cast its light over the clear sky. The fire did not, however, flash portentously and heaven was not shaken with thunder, as is the case when revelatory portents in the sky threaten the earth with a grim year of disease or war or bloodshed. Rather, shining with rays and bright with joyous light, it displayed to the amazed camp a dazzling fire. The dark shadows departed, the closer stars gave way, and their glitter, once it was effaced, lay hidden among the ruddier constellations. At first the men were astounded; the strangeness terrified all and struck fear into them. But then, little by little, their enjoyment of the light commended its celestial glow to their love.

Now, more than half the night had spun the hours along, and the wheeling day was pressing on, as the fate it would bring drew near. Then, in full view, the column was seen to move across the sky, setting the people's course as they followed it with their eyes. The holy fathers of the nation realized at once that it should be followed, that it was in fact a leader of leaders. And so, taking it as their principal guide, they joyfully put an end to delay and earnestly prepared to leave the camp. Then, after each unit had been assigned its duty, it set out in formation and the rest of the population followed.

While these things were taking place, the light of day returned and bathed heaven with brilliance. As the sun appeared, the flaming column grew pale. All the fire that had shone within it was transformed into a cloud. And yet, the appearance of its elongated form remained constant above the crystalline vault of the sky. The third hour had now dispersed the nocturnal mists, and the sun, climbing upward, had erased the morning's shadows. Then, behold, something amazing occurred: the cloud, preserved in the clear sky, was ordered to place its cooling presence in the path of the sun's hot rays and, although exceedingly thin itself, to provide an impenetrable shield of protection. And so, surrounded by the heat with which the East burns, the Hebrew throng did not experience the scorching temperature common to that land. You would have imagined that the column was scattering gentle evening breezes over them or that the moist winds were spreading a refreshing coolness around the host. And the shape that produced the cloud was not one suffused with foul color, not one so horrible in its matted aspect that it terrified the people, as is the case when clouds produce mighty storms. Rather, the towering appearance of that beautiful column was like a moist rainbow gazing at the sun. It was a fire at night and, when kindled, brought them light, but when the sun scorched them, it provided the moisture of a cool dew. Its very nature produced these changes, bringing to each part of the day an alternating boon, and its seemingly contradictory substance rendered a harmonious service with its own gifts. If it stood still, the men stood still; if it moved they followed. And if it was ordered to linger in one place for several days, the army would set up its defenses and hold its obedient ranks in bivouac.

That divine mercy was multiplied, O Jew, for forty years during which you made your way across the vast and remote parts of the desert, and the very road you travelled hardened the shoes bound to your feet. During that long period, your garments were not worn away, but remained heavy and strong. Indeed, the life of that old but enduring clothing would be long and would possess a strange softness because age would be unable to do it harm. Shining manna would provide holy food for your people, and earth's realm would behold the bread of Heaven. A sublime figure, using this manna as its vehicle, would foreshadow the fact that a pure body would one day be born of a womb untouched by human seed and that from it a meal of salvation would claim nourishment from Heaven itself, as God made His descent to our holy altars. And as part of this sign, the high priest also struck a rock and produced a watery draught for the thirsting people. From this you can see that Christ takes on for us the consistency of a hard rock and that, when struck by the lance, He offers us abundant water and provides drink for His people from His holy wound.

Now the Hebrews, with the column as their guide, joyfully traversed the land with their feet and the heavens with their eyes. But see, once again anger settled upon the Egyptians' minds, and that savage and uncouth people, even as their death approached, forged one final madness, crying out: "Alas for the error that carries too far the mockery of foolish minds! Alas for the illusions it presents with its all too cloudy deception! Is it not a shame that without a struggle an enslaved people should be rescued in this way, without paying any penalty? With what mighty divinity as the leader of their troops do these settlers leave, abandoning an empty land? The fields are deserted; the towns, their walls begun, are left unfinished. Normal work does not go forward. No farmer in his fields plies his sturdy hoe with its worn edge. The task master has grown idle and silent and there is no hubbub as raucous whippings exact their customary quota. Rather, let our army take up arms and march against them. Let it bring back their unwarlike folk and fugitive offspring. If the boldness of slaves has so kindled in them the desire for armed conflict, let their whole army die at once, mingled with their common folk. As our weapons grow hot, let even their mothers perish, along with them, their hearts pierced, and let our arrows pin their children tight to their breasts. Let each see her own child fall before her eyes and then, offering her neck, pray to meet death herself. Let their final lot make this nation taste our grief, when they have been deprived of their young. And as they lose everything in life, let them perish in the same way. Let the battlefield lie hidden beneath the dense carnage and commit their unburied bodies to the grim sky. Then let our victorious right hand, when it has satisfied all our fury with the sword, bring back the treasures that now elude us."

With blasts like these they sharpened an anger already keen, even as God mocked them, God, Who alone discerns all attempts that contemplate with an unyielding pride what cannot be, God, Who brings to nought the plans of great men and topples all their work. And yet, they demanded war. Their hot-headed young soldiers seized their weapons, the horses, mouths foaming, were led out, and shining harnesses drew in the swift teams of powerful beasts decked with brazen ornaments. The parade of warriors glistened in the sun as they pulled the axles fitted beneath their cars with golden poles. Still other soldiers were clad in steel or girded with yellow brass. These were confident beneath the great protection of their corslets, which many tightly linked rings covered, and their garments of chain-mail jingled on their bodies. On others a thin metal sheet was fitted tightly around, where it had to bend and mount through successive connected edges, all of it forming a frame made of woven metal, which, shaped as it was in this different manner, gave them a horrible guise. But among all the armaments of those eager warriors their own visages were even more terrifying, for who could look upon them in their rage, men whose faces, even when they are happy, can scarcely be beheld? Now those faces were enclosed by helmets, and iron garments circled the darkness of their wrath with the gleam of arms. The assembled army set out. The king himself whipped his neighing horses from his chariot, but on every side a wall of weapons hid him as the spears of his army formed a thick forest. The earth was shaken as it was struck by the chariot wheels and the heavy burden they bore, and the tightly-packed crowd of men made the broad earth narrow and clogged its roads. Whatever power Egypt could muster the death that was approaching drew to itself.

In the meantime the Hebrew people had advanced their army to the Red Sea, to the place where Magdalus looms above the water. They were carefree and believed that they had escaped from the enemy until, as they settled down and made ready to take their rest within the defenses they had built, they beheld clouds of dust rising into the sky. Then, before long, the encamped army caught its first sight of the savage enemy column. The approach of evening, however, and the setting of the sun did not permit the hostile forces to join battle, and the tyrant settled behind his own fortifications and put off the war until morning. And yet, Fate would not even then have restrained his burning rage and his fury would not have brooked keeping a truce even for a night. No, he would have set his standards in motion and anticipated daybreak, had not the flaming column taken its stand behind the Hebrews and, standing as a barrier between them, kept the two nations apart. The king himself, however, as he looked upon that miraculous light, feared its fire, because his own senses seethed with heat and he himself was on fire. There was after all no advantage in their dying slowly; they were destined for a single destruction, which would close upon all of them as the sea spread open.

The Hebrew people, penned up in that place, trembled and awaited in fear the destruction they thought the following day would bring. They took up no arms, engaged in no hostile exchanges, but with voices raised they harangued their priests, crying, "Three and four times blest are those whom Egypt received when they died, and blessed are those dead too for whom in its wide land it provided a funeral urn when their final lot was cast. They were indeed deemed worthy of escaping the pangs of this mighty grief and the sight of the slaughter or capture of their children. But we will be given to the birds for food, and our bodies, deprived of burial, will decay in this vast desert." So the men spoke, and the entire host responded with lamentation as the crowd ranged through the camp and the confusion grew.

Then the holy leaders of the Hebrew people began to recall what had been promised and with these words soothed their fears and wiped away the people's tears. "We beseech you," they said, "to put out of your minds these ungrateful fears. After all you have experienced, do not imagine that all the gifts Heaven promises with these mighty portents are to be despaired of. Is it possible for Egypt to escape from our faithless hearts, stricken as it is with so much misfortune and sinking beneath a lash even the earth felt, when you and all that is yours lived in safety so long under the rule of this battered enemy? Why should we speak of what has happened already? Surely you see that the protection of the column, our link with God, looks after us, so that we need not fear anything from the enemy's deceit. Rather, with an unwavering hope, lift up your spirits and keep them high, for tomorrow has been fixed as the last for that nation, which, as it rattles swords, puts its faith in the arms it has taken up. That is not the kind of war we face. You will not carry weapons against weapons, nor will triumph come to you in this turn of events through your own effort. The wrath of Heaven will have to be contended with. With it and with nothing more than an untroubled nod from the Lord your battle tomorrow will be concluded."

With words like these their diligent priests lifted up the dejected hearts of the people and calmed their fears with their holy voices. Throughout the night a strong wind with hot gusts kept burning the sea and consuming the deep, for the Almighty Father, contrary to nature's rules sent flame upon the waters, and the waves beneath his breath caught fire in the troubled gulf. Now the shimmering edge of day had just made its way to morning, and the bright dawn was scattering its first ruddy light over the world. Then all at once the Egyptians burst out of their foul camp, and their soldiers, once set in motion, raised the battlecry on every side. After it reached the ears of the frightened Hebrew people and the trumpets' blast had struck their hearts with terror, they took to the road and followed it to where the nearby margin of the sea, now emptied of its red water, beckoned them.

When the people reached the very edge of the sea, the waves were drawn back in reverent obedience and, giving way at once, opened up a path for those to whom the enemy denied access to the land. A structure, which a wall of hanging water had created, held the sea back and kept it suspended in the air. God's chosen people marched straight into the gap as they fled and confounded their pursuers by walking on land in the middle of the sea. The stones of the deep were trodden upon and the tracks of their wagons wore down the exposed mud. The hot sun thrust its glance between the separated waves and touched with strange light land unknown before. Its lengthened rays struggled to descend to such a depth, and its weary glow reached the seabed only with difficulty.

At first the Pharaoh imagined that the Hebrews had been blocked and driven back by the waves and that they had turned their backs in retreat. With these words he ordered his army to shake off any further delay. "Behold," he cried, "their fleeing troops once again quit the battle that threatens and, placing their trust in the safety their nimble feet can find, make their retreat. Hem them round with your arms. Just keep the pressure on them and, once they are surrounded, the sea will do the rest." Scarcely had he finished speaking when his soldiers leapt up and rushed toward the shore. When they reached it, they saw that a vast expanse of waterless deep had provided an unusual path, that an avenue of retreat had opened up in a way that made it appear that the waves had fled in fear from the tread of the holy nation. And the Egyptians saw that they could safely descend along that dry track without concern for the sea or themselves, without fear of enemy arms or of the sea, which rankled little under its strange constraint. The army came to a halt and stood motionless for a while. Tugging at their reins, they restrained the teams of horses, and then some man to whose heart a kindled spark gave a feeble fire, happened to call out: "What God twists the world from its ancient hinge, alters its orderly behavior with a new law and throws into confusion all that He has built? For if the nature of each created thing abides, what then is the cause of this monstrous path? And if the sea can be crossed on foot, what remains at last but for fields to be ploughed by ships, for Heaven to drop down from its own vault, for Hell to be raised up to Heaven, for the hot regions of the sky to grow cold and the Scorpion to set the Bear aflame with its blast? What remains but to believe that some confusion in the order of nature turns these things upside down? No one will descend into this desiccated sea with me as his leader. No, let this path which guides our enemy be suspect as far as I am concerned, for if the divinity who balances the scales of fate wanted a fair war, he would have maintained this barrier and blocked that fleeing army. Now let them go, and let those portents of theirs follow that vagabond nation alone. I for one will have nothing to do with the sea that surrounds this deep cleft and conceals whatever dangers may lurk on its now exposed floor." But the violent crowd, on fire with discordant ideas, took exception to his words, and the hidden sentence of their approaching death drove them on.

That renowned nation had now marched beyond the valley of water. Leaving behind the gathered billows of the empty gulf, they climbed up the rising dunes beyond the abyss. The commander of the black army was beside himself, and rage took hold of the Pharaoh, whose own name was Cencres. Then, just as the Hebrews had done, the Egyptians entered the trench in the parted sea and rushed along its path. What will mad fury not dare? One part of the cavalry drove its column forward beside the army; another whipped its teams and ordered its swift chariots to ride beyond the main body of troops. As a result, the impatient horsemen, angry and hot for battle, reached the middle of the sea first and began to curse the delay that the broad gulf was causing, as their slower companions behind them trembled in the narrow world they had entered. At that moment, a voice, was broadcast from the sky, through that lofty column in its bright cloud, and the bearer of the word of Heaven cried out, calling the holy leader Moses by name. "The time has come," it said, "in which My commitment to you can be made good. Now the end of Egypt is at hand. Now with one final letting of blood My sentence of destruction will punish this nation that has been castigated in so many ways already. Now let the sword follow upon the lash. Just strike the divided waters with your rod, and the sea will return and assume again its own appearance."

Moses knelt down and, with faith in the mysterious power of his remarkable rod, struck the edge of the desiccated coast, struck the very shore, in order to make the waves that had deserted it return again at his command. Thereupon a sudden crash rippled through the air above and cascading water thundered on every side. The waves first came together at the place where his final fate was revealing a path to the Pharaoh. After that path had been closed, however, and the waves drove him back as he rode along, he indeed regretted having entered the gulf and, fleeing, strove too late to return. The frightened troops turned their backs and threw away their weapons. The sea pursued them as they fled and relentlessly came to meet them. On all sides the surrounding wall of water rushed down and, with nothing to hold it back, collapsed upon them. He who had always been savage, now grew gentle in the moment of death and cried out: "This victory does not yield to human struggle. We are routed and overcome by a heavenly enemy. Flee, my conquered attendants, flee and escape whichever of you can. Do not at this point cast your weapons against God in a futile trial of strength." O, if only human pride were willing before its destruction to change its ways when it is stung by conscience. What good is it, after all, to put an end to evil-doing when the end of life presses upon us, when the span of our present existence yields to time? "Confess," say the strong and healthy in Scripture, for if anyone vows to be done with his sins when he is no longer able to sin, he is himself undone by his self-indulgence.

And so, the enemy phalanx, on the very point of drowning, was lifted up and hung suspended on the rising waves. Because of the weight of their weapons, however, they sank into the rising mountain of water, and their dying bodies bore their iron clothing to the sticky bottom. Some freed themselves of their armaments first and then wrapped their swimming limbs around one another in a sad embrace until, cheated of rescue, they perished, for as they clasped each other for mutual support, they sank down and died with arms and legs inter-twined. Still others, tossing their weary arms about for a long time, ran onto swords or hung upon floating lances, and the like-colored sea mingled with their red blood.

Prominent among them, the prince of Memphis' halls, guiding with his black driver a white team of horses, witnessed the slaughter of his own people and, as the last survivor, was shipwrecked in his chariot by the attacking waves. There was no real war, for the water did battle, and Israel, without stirring itself, emerged victorious, having seen the strug-gle to its end with its eyes alone. Then the valley of the sea was filled and disappeared. As the waves flowed back, the surface of the level gulf extended far and wide again. Foul corpses were thrown up on the entire length of its shore, and the sea made a show of its triumph over the land.

The renowned leader of the Hebrews described this remarkable event in that hymn of celebration which is now recited throughout the world, when guilt is purged and washed away by baptism and the waters that bring life-giving cleansing produce new offspring to replace the guil-ty men of old whom Eve bore, Eve, whom my slender page made its subject earlier in my text, when it recounted that grievous fall. But whatever grim events have been narrated in this poor verse, these too will have been cleansed by the memorable water of that holy triumph in which joys resound, by which all sins are taken away, through whose purgation the new man lives as the old dies, from which all good arises and by which deadly deeds are slain, by whose holy waters the true Israel is washed, in which a harmonious throng rejoices and celebrates

its victory and in which are fulfilled the figures that foreshadowed fu-
ture gifts, figures which the holy prophet explained in his five volumes.
We follow his trumpet with our reed pipe and, respecting the number
of his books, we shall make a port for our small bark upon this shore.

## Prologue 2

To my holy Lord and brother, Apollinaris, Bishop, most pious and
blessed, greetings from his brother in Christ, Alcimus Avitus.

My first poems have now appeared, published not so much through
my own efforts, although that was my wish, as through the lively initia-
tive, kindly if somewhat unexpected, which you and some of your as-
sociates took. Now, in addition, you urge me specifically to send you
those verses that I wrote for our admirable sister, Fuscina, on the subject
of the consolatory praise that chastity earns. When I sent you word that
I had finished this work, I was inclined, more correctly I think, to refer
to it as a short verse. You, however, in your first response called it a
book, suggesting, I suppose, that that term was appropriate in view of its
length. This being the case, be assured that I shall follow your judge-
ment, or shall I say your graciousness, in this regard too, for it is surely
wrong for me to contradict in small things one whom I obey in great.
I would ask, however, that, devoted brother that you are, you recall that
the work you call a little book treats in a rather intimate manner with
the religious sensibilities of our parents and the virgin women of our
family and should, therefore, be placed in the hands of those alone
whom either family bonds or common religious practices truly link
with us. You can judge from the nature of the material, which was
composed for a sister in private and saintly meditation and divulged to
you only after I was moved by your frequent requests, when and in
what manner I would want it to reach the hands of those outside our
circle of family and friends. You realize that I was on the point of
abandoning the composition of poetry or verse on any new subjects and
would have done so, had not a clear and compelling reason turned me
away from this resolve and toward the need for a short poem of this
sort. And it *is* a short poem. I promise that you will find it so slight that
even you will not presume to apply to it any other name. Indeed, for
some time our calling and, more recently, our years have suggested that
it is proper for us, if we must take pen in hand, to spend our time and
effort on more serious literary themes, not squandering further days on

a work that charms a few knowledgeable people by preserving a metrical pattern, but composing instead a work that serves many readers with its measured instruction in the faith.

## 6. On Virginity

Virgin, eminently worthy of Christ, take and hold these gifts which your brother Alcimus sends you. In these trifling verses find weighty arguments, and, as you do, let this slight poem commend my brave love. For as often as you complete your round of holy duties, that responsive and melodious singing of the psalms, which the living harp in your heart adapts to modest harmonies, using its own musical power and the chords within it, then may you open my poem, take delight and relieve your weary mind in meditation. This lyre is not tainted by the waters of falsehood, in whose accounts Pegasus is imagined outstripping the swift winds in his movements and then, after taking flight, whinnying in mid-air, as the hooves of a mighty horse are carried along on nimble wings. Nor do the Sisters whom tradition deceives itself by calling three times three inspire my songs in the trivial Pierian fashion, but truthful music presents you with a brother's plectrum true, and this, our pipe, echoing Christ, will be immune to Phoebus' inspiration.

When your mother, Audentia, bore a fourth child, and produced you, rich as she was in children, as her final offspring, she promised at the same moment to live a life of self-denial. Thereafter, her dear parents' zeal dedicated them to chastity with similar vows. And because you were the beginning of a compact so holy, you were offered to Christ with her, and He at once received your infant limbs even in your hallowed cradle. In the same way, long ago, when the bright earth was young and shone with new vegetation, when its seeds produced luscious fruits, Abel, the just, led a new-born animal alive to the holy altars and, as faith stole upon him, recognized that the lamb with its innocent bleating had raised a cry to God. And so, through the sacrifice of that one creature the entire flock became pleasing to the Lord. Later, when the waters of life-giving baptism nurtured you, and heavenly grace produced what had been pledged to it, they set no necklaces on a neck bejewelled, nor did you wear a robe shining with woven gold and containing threads of finely spun precious metal. No Sidonian purple from shellfish twice boiled clothed you, no brilliant vermilion from ruby dyes, none of the soft silks China exports. They did not pierce your ears and fix in them gold clasps from which pearls are hung to grace the

wounds and, however precious, to lie heavy, being stone after all, on a
maiden's cheeks. Blessed Isaiah described these things more fully and
tells of the various ornaments that grace limbs soon to provide food for
worms, perhaps even while life remains in them. For no one can re-
count in words the many dreaded risks of disease we all learn to fear be-
fore our death. Better to say perhaps that we learn that our individual
parts are subject to every kind of death, while all bodies find their own
final dissolution, as one sickness carries the day and all of the rest re-
treat. But see how, nevertheless, each person longs to deck himself in an
elegance doomed to perish, while the inner man is foul and debases him-
self in sin.

But when your years reached ten, then, before long, the white stole
graced you with its simple elegance, as did a virgin's face and a becom-
ing mien. Although in its first bloom, your mind now matured and con-
ceived a sense of modesty in all its thoughts. In the same way, another
woman, although barren, with her youth behind her, rejoiced in preg-
nancy and, after giving birth to an unexpected child, happily wove for
her son a small garment so that even as a boy Samuel would learn that
he was a priest. Similarly your own happy home prepared you for the
holy altars and taught you to grow up worthy of the temple it knew so
well. You are enrolled as consort, are wedded to a mighty King, and
Christ wants to join Himself to your beautiful form, which He has se-
lected and which His potent grace makes rich with adornments of all
kinds. When your mother, experiencing these joys, came and saw the
great blessing that had been conferred on you in your youth, in those
tender years when we put our faith in virtue, she bore you again in a
way far better than she had in her womb. Both hope and fear were hers
and, although now free of the vow she made for you, she gave you this
advice, mingling tears with her pleas because even in her joy she re-
mained anxious, enduring as she was unsettling worries on your behalf:
"My sweet child, born fourth but first in grace, you whom I bore twice
to Heaven, in flesh and in faith, you whom I dedicated as an infant to
Christ, the past has been ours to live together, but now, with the pass-
ing of years, it is proper that your vow be your own. That vow of vir-
ginity you received originally from me, but now you will begin to exer-
cise your own power over everything since everything is yours to will.
The footsteps along the path you will be following in your ascent to
Heaven are still warm, and models abound in your family. See how
many crowns our line, which blossoms with virgins, has sent to Heaven,
the crowns which mother Severiana holds up as a holy lesson, praying

that you will be joined with them. Years ago, when she was not much older than you, Aspidia joyfully veiled her blessed head and took up duties like yours by committing her twelve years to the holy altars. Her final destiny may indeed have permitted a sudden death to snatch her away from us, but such a departure is never sudden for those who are always prepared. And now see the very high point, shining as your virgin twin, our greatest glory in whose name, you, Fuscina, recall, as descendent, that Fuscina of old. And with the same eagerness recall another strong in piety, one who in the Greek name she assumed suggested the quality of her own mind. Grant, therefore, that the ages they lived in accorded to them the pre-eminence they deserved and that their lives surpassed all others given the lofty pinnacle of sanctity they achieved. But if in your noble heart you follow these women, your ancestors will rejoice to be surpassed, as you advance. They will willingly give you the palm of victory for going beyond even the prayers of your teacher." With these words she kindled a girl's love of virginity and stirred her tender sensibilities with her holy encouragement. In the same way that famous mother, mighty Machabaea, who brought forth life in her womb but greater life in her deeds, actually rejoiced in the death of a child, rejoiced with mind victorious that her old age was deprived; and so, teaching her child not to yield to the enticements of the world, she set afire a holy passion for heroic works. Why should I repeat now the reply you made with greater courage than your tender age would warrant and with a wisdom unusual for your years? This short poem has not undertaken your praise. In the fullness of time death, the conqueror, will come, and your praise will be better sung when, amid cries of triumph, your deeds will receive their full reward. What we ought to do now, awed as we are, is to caution and advise you, think upon your concerns and share your anxieties, let our words of encouragement help you to endure your labors while, as danger follows danger, every kind of catastrophe assails you, while your uncertain life continues along a precarious path, while the serpent, which has been trodden upon and which any foot that mounts the high road of righteousness may bruise, dogs your steps. For this present existence offers nothing certain, and no rest from care is granted to those who wear this dying flesh. Often the good are brought low, virtue is vanquished and perishes, and the rewards of glory achieved in the past recede from view. Often the mind, lately cold, is wont to be set afire with a sudden religious fervor, to withdraw from the world and with reins hidden until then put a stop to its sins. This is the way fate changes, turning now this way, now that, so that the unholy man may hope for forgiveness and the just profit from fear and add a final capstone to the great virtue he has practiced. For if it happens that zeal in holy works is relaxed and if a lazy indolence undoes our customary prudence, then the glory of a life, doomed in the end, falls headlong away. Merit cannot stand still. If it does not increase as it advances, it is diminished in its retreat. We must struggle with great effort to keep our steps on the narrow path. For the man who takes his pleasure in worldly things, while the distance before him spreads out in a wide and open road, runs now along an easy path, but a narrower cell will imprison him when his cruel fate is accomplished.

All I ask is that you pardon the love of him who exhorts you, who counsels a runner when he can scarcely follow himself. This is surely a case of a sluggard who has taken a short-cut prompting one who is swift. You come to the instruction I offer in my poor verse with greater understanding now, you who, though younger in years, dedicated yourself to the discipline of the religious life first and, although subordinate when years alone are counted, excel in merit. If we, your kin, are followers with you, our action may at present be reckoned our own, but in fact our following comes from you, for the change in your brothers' lives is due to your own holy example. Your Author makes you His concern and in you presents the first fruits of His blessed harvest, but remember our holy faith reveals that a burden shared in the spirit of family love can lighten a brother's load too. You, my sister, hold on your devoted shoulder the holy burden which you brought from your mother's breast, not according to the flesh but the law, you who are bent to bear a yoke but not to accept the bonds of marriage. You have chosen to hate the ways of the tainted world and to walk among the untainted, denying yourself the marriage bed of the former, seeking Christ as a spouse among the latter. You have chosen to spurn the torches of marriage but to glow with a holy love, to be sluggish in passion but afire in your heart for work. You have chosen to be ignorant of man and to produce the kind of offspring that no sad misfortune can ever take away.

You will not weep when deprived of the pledges of your fecund life, nor fear to survive as widow your constant spouse, yourself free from evil. Nor are you touched by the emotion that overcame Eve, the mother of both offspring and of death that day she bore a dead child and with it a guilt that lived on afterwards. She was subject to a man and doomed to suffer a master in her chamber. She served in a disgusting bed, as she endured wedlock. You see how a woman is really a captive, although she bears the empty name of wife and in a hollow charade is called a consort and equal. But beneath that yoke she is forced to endure an unequal lot all by herself, and when a long and loathsome malaise fills out ten months, her heavy stomach is stretched by the fully formed child that was its father's seed. As her womb swells, this burden inflicts terrible pain upon its mother, for when she is unburdened and the birth is difficult, one alone pays the price, at great peril to her own flesh, and makes good for what two did together. Perhaps hope comforts her as she grieves, if only the son she bears should live. But it often happens that as she groans she gives birth to dead children. And often the dead limbs of a mother assign a double tomb to an offspring never born because of death's intervention. And how often does that less terrible thing occur, that the mother herself dies alone and, after bringing forth her burden, gives up both the child and her ghost? What if it happens that a child, raised and nourished year after year, is carried off by death, one on whom, again and again, a mother's one hope rested? Then everything is gone, everything her joys promised her when she framed her prayers. And a case more dreadful than all of these occurs when envious death snatches away a tender child who lacks baptism and who must be borne under that harsh sentence to Hell. Such a child, when it ceases to be the child of its mother, becomes the son of damnation, and its sad parents wish unborn the limbs to which they gave life only to see them consigned to the flames. Who could possibly recall the perils bred of all those misfortunes by which pride in beloved flesh is betrayed? But under the rule by which you are now bound, a new freedom has the power to move your life to a place distant and remote from these things, and as a result the unholy bonds of the false world do not hold you fast. You follow Mary, who was permitted under Heaven's dispensation to rejoice in the twin crown, that of both virgin and mother, when she conceived God in the flesh, and the Creator of Heaven, revealing the mystery of His being, entered her inviolate womb. He would be His mother's child, but He chose to enter the world in a pure womb which He Himself had formed. He alone arranged the birth of His own flesh, knew the day from afar and spied out the time in which He was to be brought forth. His will preceded His body. God Himself assumed our flesh as the Word's clothing, and He Who rules with the Father served in a mother's body and, as the Lord had commanded, accepted the life of a servant. From His Father He received no knowledge of passing time, from His mother no seed of generation. And yet, she was indeed full of life who deserved to carry her own Maker as an unblemished burden and to bring forth her eternal Lord. But you, my sister, will not be without the glory of a deed that great if, as you conceive Christ in your faithful heart, you produce for Heaven the holy blossoms of good works. "If anyone," He says, "rightly fulfills Our law, he will always be father, mother and sister to Me." You see then how Heaven's aspect, which the chosen man within grasps intellectually, is without sex. The Savior, when He arose from the dead, gave us an example when He gave greater honor to women than to men. Christ was tasting the death He underwent for our sins, hanging, although guiltless, on that tall cross, and, pierced with nails, He breathed from His holy lips the soul that would soon return to His living limbs. Then the crowd of onlookers fled from that sight, for they could not endure the portents with which the gloomy sky threatened them. The sun was shrouded, and turned its face away from the earth. It granted to that night of grief hours not its own and permitted an alien darkness to approach. As this change of time occurred in the great order of the universe, night fell upon the realms above and the world below saw light. The earth shook, and under this great pressure its walls tottered as their crests were struck at their very peaks. Rocks, when ordered to leave the places where they had lain so long, felt motion and produced strange sounds as they clashed against one another. With this thunder in their ears, as everyone else fled, those famous women, in spite of their fear, decided to stand fast, to act as a watch and secure the holy tomb with the devotion of the living, decided to be there and to pay it honor with their prayers. They laid out expensive bolts of linen rinsed in fragrant juices, to preserve a body both saving and saved. Their love prepared these sad gifts at their own expense and out of a sense of obligation to the dead. When, however, Christ averted the need for these things in an instant by His Resurrection, He was moved nonetheless by the gift thought necessary to preserve the dead but in fact not needed by Him. And so, in return for it, a grace at once granted that human eyes should behold an angelic countenance. A brilliant robe shone upon the angel's heavenly body and a fiery glow suffused his entire countenance, in order that, once seen, he might speak Heaven's message to those worthy women, letting the following words fall from his holy lips: "In your woman's sex excel even a man's mind and do not allow yourselves, brave hearts, to be seized by a new panic. These portents are meant for your enemies. You no longer have any cause to fear, you whom a holy love's zeal has made steadfast. I know that you seek within the precinct of this precious tomb for Jesus, Who was lately buried here with solemn rites. But you should remember what He said before He died, knowing the future as He did and being incapable of falsehood. He said that He was not to be held in death's clutches for more than two nights. And now the third day, the one that fulfills His promise, has come. Behold, the tomb lies open. Rising again, He has left it empty in His victory over death."

In these words the messenger from Heaven delivered the speech he had been ordered to give, destined as he was to lavish on earth the gifts which Christ's life-giving victory had produced. He granted those women the first joy mankind would feel and relieved their sorrow. And so, unafraid, their breasts now filled with happiness, they walked away, pressing to their hearts the belief that their salvation had been accomplished. And Christ appeared in their midst as they went along, bade them to recognize Him and gave them a greeting. "Go," He said, "and bring this message to My disciples so that they may know that their Master has risen." The women embraced His feet and placed kisses upon them. Then they ran eagerly to the disciples and gave those learned men instruction. And they in turn, after having been taught by women's words, which would be spread throughout all the world, recognized that mind and not gender carried off the palm of victory.

It follows that virtue and danger are common to both men and women. There is no difference in our hearts. Each is capable of willing what is right if grace is present. To attain this, however, the lives of either sex must sweat and never rest from the struggle. For what good are God's gifts to man if, with a mind irresolute, both sluggish and lazy, he fritters away the privilege he has been granted? Struggle loves help but who will aid a lazy man or wed virtue and torpid sleep?

The King of Heaven, as *He* was preparing to leave the earth, gave silver to *His* servants, each according to his merit, five minae to the first, two to the second and to the third, whose accomplishments were not as great, a single mina. Then as He departed, He instructed all His servants together, saying, "Now, so that I may learn which of you is faithful and devoted, let me discover from the way you use this money what powers each of you possesses and with what skills you are endowed. Double this investment of mine, make it shine brighter in use and let no dull surface stain it with dark rust. You are receiving a shining coin with an unmarked face. When I come back, you will be rewarded according to your just desserts." So He spoke and departed for His heavenly kingdom. Two of the servants put their whole minds to the question of the money and contended with one another in zealously putting it to use. One was quick to increase his portion of the gleaming treasure by gener-

ously giving most of it to the poor, and whatever he gave to the needy
grew and was gathered into great piles. The second, who spent his ef-
forts in explaining the mysteries of the holy Word, rejoiced to see his in-
terest grow and reaped a holy profit. Eager for righteousness, he confer-
red eternal life on his listeners as he preached. But the servant who had
received the coin of least value remained all by himself and buried his
purse in a ditch he had dug, choosing to live without principles in de-
generate self-indulgence. At last, when the world came to an end, their
Judge returned and the foolish servant looked with contempt on that re-
turn, whose putting off had been of no concern to him. Then the Lord,
wanting them to give an accounting, ordered them all to show what re-
turn the occupations they had busied themselves with would bring Him
when, after so long a time, He asked for a report. The two servants
whose treasure had doubled presented their silver and rendered up their
wares with a smile. The third, who was lazy, presented the coin that had
lain hidden in the ground and that, having soaked up the contagion of
the mud around it, had lost its natural appearance because of the crust
on its bright surface. Then the Lord chastised him in a terrifying voice.
"Is this how little you thought of Me, loafing here? Is this how little
you worried about My return, lazy servant? Look how you now return
foul and covered with rust, the silver you received from Me pure and
shining! The engraving I once recognized has vanished and no longer
looks like Me as it once did. Now the image of My countenance does
not resemble the one entrusted to you. If you had devoted what was en-
trusted to you to the service of My altars and if it had reached that
table, then the coin inscribed with Our name would have increased.
Now then, My faithful servants, take everything and let the final distri-
bution award to the industrious what it takes from the lazy, for this rep-
robate will be worthy of not even the smallest favor. Whoever knowing-
ly despises his Lord's will, is punished much; he who sins in ignorance
only a little."

Therefore, my sister, rise and come with limbs girt for the brave
fight. Come armed in your mind and do not as a woman fear the war
that the mind must fight. You have long known from your frequent
reading the glory of your sex. I cannot imagine that you feel self-doubt
when you consider how Deborah once led the battalions drawn up be-
hind a brave trumpet, how a woman, taking up her standard, marched
before the army and exhorted the astonished men whom she guided
with her words and the example of her leadership, as she set their fight-
ing spirit afire. After that brave captain took the lead, after she had set

alight arms already instinct with fury and urged her companies on, the horde of barbarians fell and the enemy power was completely dissolved. Wherever the woman appeared, the foemen broke ranks and turned their backs. They made for places to hide and considered it a victory merely to save their lives. Then the mighty king himself, Sisarra, to whom nature had given a gigantic stature and a head that towered above all others, threw aside the burden of his weapons and took flight without a guard, fearing that his great body would be recognized and that his towering frame would betray him as he fled. And yet, even as he imagined that he was concealed, even when he had reached a shelter, he closed his tired eyes in the sleep that never ends, for a woman killed him too, and her hammer pierced his temples with the nail it drove into them as he lay on the ground. And so it happened that that triumph belonged entirely to women. But you, maiden of God, with your saintly demeanor, embellished here by modesty, there by faith, you are braver still and wage war with the soul's weaponry. Yours are the wars that our cruel enemy unleashes on the just. Let hope bred of faith sit as the helmet of victory on your head and let the girdle of precious modesty enfold your limbs. Let the tunic of justice be wrapped around your cloak and let the clear message of the Word be always in your hand to act as your sword. In describing the various battles that the mind wages with the body, Prudentius once prudently wrote of these powers of virtue, these comforts in war. Indeed, in his work the warrior maid, Virginity, came forward, armed and powerful in the fullness of her might. Foul desire pursued her and vainly endeavored to challenge her to fight. I hope the jealous snake will find you such a warrior when you are challenged, and when battle grants you the palm, I hope that you will joyfully accept victory's first prize from the enemy you trod upon.

Keep in mind as well whatever holy message the divine Scriptures teach with eloquence and insight, the things which that ancient author Moses proclaimed as he revealed the beginnings of the world, weaving his tale now in narrative, now in figurative speech, also what of importance was accomplished in the past, after Ruth's time, in the various reigns of those many monarchs as they gave way to one another. And remember the psalms three times fifty that King David wrote in verse after the rule of Saul, the reprobate, and whatever Solomon, the peacemaker, composed in his broad kingdom, using unambiguous proverbs to express his obscure meaning. Keep in mind too what the sixteen prophets who followed him saw and what hidden message long-suffering Job proclaimed, his wounds still gaping wide. Why should I recall Hester and the lies of Judith, the pure, who, when the governor of her land grew hot with desire at the sight of her powdered face's false promise, remained to mock his filthy couch and put an end to his brutish leer by cutting off his head? Keep in mind what Tobit wrote, keener than others in vision although physically blind, and the secret things the author Esdras saw and wrote down and finally all those things that grace, which replaced the old law, thunders forth along with the miracles of the New Testament which the face of man proclaims in one book, but which the face of the lion, the swift eagle and the bull that is brave in his contest proclaim in others. Do not forget what the twelve lambs, the Disciples pure in spirit, did, spreading the seeds of their wisdom throughout the world, what the fourteen Epistles of St. Paul proclaimed far and wide, what Peter and Jacob teach us, what Jude wrote and John himself, who tells the secrets of Heaven he saw, yes, and all the worthy mysteries those truthful authors set down in their books. You have, I know, kept these things in your mind and have drunk with a thirsty spirit. And now, if our own poets write of anything holy, do not let these things escape your notice. You understand syntax and metrics, can read a phrase properly and so can add grace to another's verse as you read. What need is there for me to explain everything? Use the good sense your education has given you and with a manly zeal turn what you know or what you have merely skimmed in your reading into a work of virtue. For unless the life of faith is joined with learning, knowledge of things that will not be acted upon will in fact do you graver harm.

The Lord was hungry one day long ago and, as He went along, He happened to see a fig tree and its canopy of delicate leaves. It was just the right season for plucking ripe fruit from the tree He saw, but He discovered at once that it was clothed with leaves only and was barren of blossoms. In an instant that useless ornament, flourishing as it was to no end, began to tremble violently. Its roots were suddenly struck by a blast of heat, and its trunk lost the cover of its branches and dried up. By this sign we learn to know the law: that no servant of Christ should confess Him in words alone and, feigning the name of Christian, accomplish no living works. For if we consider ourselves Christians and righteous, it would make things even worse if deeds did not follow our words. And so, virginity, which is dedicated to holy modesty, needs other virtues to accompany it and, unless it preserves a mind that is pure and links that to a chaste body, it sleeps with vice and cannot rightly call chaste the flesh that an adulterous mind corrupts. Anger, madness, grief, malice, discord, luxury, duplicity, bound hands and loose will, all these play adulterer with the heart of man and then nourish from their base seed the child of death. See to what end each is led who, while flaunting virginity, fails to realize that a mind heavy with sin swells up within her. Look, here is one example by which you may recognize other cases.

One day when the Lord happened to be teaching the people how, by watching zealously they might recognize the final hour and await the day on which the world's judge would draw near, He compared those marked with the holy chrism to virgins and cited at the top of His list of examples those ten well-known maidens, five of whom a rich wisdom adorned while the senses of the others had been bent to stupidity by their laziness. A single repose embraced them all in their weariness, and sleep, which is the sign of death, pressed upon their eyes. Midnight had just passed for the sleepers and it was that time of night, Hell, when Christ Who had taken on our flesh, broke the barrier of your gates and shattered the hinge of death, that time when, after spurning His tomb, He returned in joyous light from the darkness He had overcome. It was at that hour that a sudden cry rang out and broke the silence: "The bridegroom is here at last. Shake from your bodies the night's sluggishness, and let your limbs spurn your couch and be nimble." They all got up at once and left their beds. Searching for their lamps, they adjusted their flames. Then the five who were cleverer, although they were in a hurry, took care nevertheless to add oil to the lamps they picked up and so they cleaved the murky night with fires fortified by the rich liquid. But the other group left the oil behind and so took up their torches and carried them in vain. A small flame shone from their lights as they waved them in the air, but the glow lacked power and failed the sputtering lamps. The flame ran along the dry papyrus, and amid rolling clouds of pitchy smoke the ashes grew white as they rose higher in a smoldering heap. When they saw that they had fallen short in their preparation, and were unworthy to meet the bridegroom who was drawing near, untimely anxiety aroused shame and grief in the lazy girls. Meekly begging in their silly voices, they asked the other five to reach over and help them in rousing their own lifeless fires, pleaded that their abundant good sense share its oil. The other maidens replied in unison with words like these: "The cause of your misfortune is indeed to be lamented, but still, each of us brought only as much oil as she needed, and so now enough remains in our lamps and just the right measure maintains the level of the liquid. It is not right to share what we went to get, not right

to waste the oil for fear that, when the fuel is portioned out, the hollow
lamps will be left empty. Don't you see that the moment all the lights
grow weak and their flames begin to wane, our loss will nonetheless
deny you any gain?" Such was their refusal, their sad denial, and so the
other girls wandered out to wherever in that place shops and merchants
were still busy. While they were gone, however, the bridegroom came
in and led the girls who were prepared into his chamber, closing the
door so that the sisters who were still wandering around were left be-
hind and excluded. You can see, then, how a virgin's honorable reputa-
tion may be lost, if her holy fire is not carried into the chambers of
Heaven. But blessed is that hand which provides itself in advance with
great gifts and tends its burning light with an oil that is pure and abun-
dant. For as much oil is poured into capacious vessels as a person in his
compassion gives to the beggar in need. In this story the Lord admonish-
es us to bear in our hands lights that burn. This is our responsibility,
this is the glory of a bright life. Therefore, let piety and patience and a
strength that is the strength of the mind be your support. For an un-
swerving resolve has sometimes raised even maidens whose flesh is weak
to Heaven.

The fame of Eugenia was celebrated in ages past throughout the
world for the manner in which she dedicated her life to Christ. Al-
though a woman, she had already made progress in brave deeds when,
surrounded by a group of saintly companions, she became an abbot, fill-
ing the role of spiritual father while concealing her maternal nature. But
after she had offered a shining example to all with the holy words she
spoke and had, although still young, given guidance to the elderly who
were heavy in years and good deeds and revered for their enduring
piety, at that moment the serpent, who can never endure righteousness
and who makes a thousand deadly schemes take fire as he prods and
pesters us, presented her with a crown even as he wanted to stain her
reputation. He roused a woman, because of her mad, girlish love, to pre-
tend that Eugenia too had felt love's flame and was afire with a man's
passion. A confused crowd of elders gathered when they learned that the
man's base intentions had been able to undo with a sin so grave a life
lately so austere. And so, deprived of its great driving spirit, Perfection
itself stumbled, and grieved to discover that there was nothing the flesh
could not accomplish. The young girl was brought to court, and now
the disguised monk, entered the cruel tribunal as well. The unhappy co-
incidence of their deceptions was carrying the day, and the people's vio-
lent temper, itself ignorant of the girl's secret, burned with an indigna-

tion so malevolent that it was on the point of finding the girl guilty. Then, recalling that she was a woman and modest in her heart, Eugenia unsaid her own deception and, as a woman, was victorious. Although compelled to confess the flesh outwardly, inwardly she was saved and remained a heroine. The protection that her vow of chastity offered her remained at all times intact. So you see that, although the shrewd duplicity of the pitiful world attacks, weaving falsehoods and grappling for souls with nets of guile, nevertheless, the mind that is ignorant of guilt suffers no headlong ruin. Those whom our raging enemy troubles with his lying craftiness suffering will refine with its holy fire when they are in need of purgation.

Once the jealous band of his brothers sold young Joseph into slavery, and the land of Memphis held him as its servant. Then indeed he suffered a mistress when, convicted under the trumped up charge that he had willed a sordid outrage that he had in fact shunned, he persevered, enduring prison, bonds and chains until the sun, traversing again the expanse of the sky, linked to his first year of imprisonment yet a second. He had forgotten what light was, and his hair, nourished by his own emaciation touched his back with its flowing locks. And yet, God kept him alive and vigorous, and his mind, which no darkness imprisoned, foresaw what hidden things his liberation would bring in time to come. When at long last he was released, the people contended with one another to honor him. Not only was he pardoned, but they begged him with prayers to agree to wear a diadem on his prisoner's head. Let him, they cried, exchange exile for sovereignty, the name of slave for a prince's title. And so it happened that he learned the rewards of a steadfast heart.

Susanna is next. Who can ever hope to honor her with the praise she deserves? Once long ago, in spite of her tender years, she overcame the improper advances of two old men and their conspiracy of passion. The idea took hold of them individually at first and each hatched a separate plan. Each independently held out for himself the hope of guilt, but the fire that burned basely in their hearts brought their two minds together in a common furnace of crime. They met by chance one day, and after first pretending to depart, returned from different directions. Together they came to a grove and openly declared in turn the common desire that burned in both their hearts. As soon as they had deceived the girl with some subterfuge or other, they took her by surprise together. They made their demand. She had better yield, they warned her, before rumor requites her stubbornness with great disgrace. Should she not give in, the evil deed could not help but be turned against her before long. They confessed their passion, together proclaimed the lies they had devised and spread out the snares with which they wanted to catch her. The girl was of two minds. She struggled with herself for some time, wavering in her hesitation about which decision her uncertain mind should make. The law forbade her to sin, and yet the possible disgrace terrified her. She tried again and again to soften their unyielding passion with her prayers, to extinguish those obscene flames with her tears. But she succeeded in getting rid of them neither with prayers nor warnings, for a kindred passion held the old men in its clutches. Then the woman, her mind afire with a splendid modesty, decided to die chaste, to keep traffic in the flesh from enveloping her poor life in a sin so grave. She called upon Heaven as witness and rejected the false reputation they threatened her with, satisfied with her own judgement, because her unblemished faith knew her own heart and dedicated and preserved itself for the life to come.

But, He Who knows all secrets preferred to provide an open investigation then and there, in order to reveal the hidden crime and bring to light the deception the men's snares had woven. A certain young man stood watching the city as it was shaken by senseless weeping. He would later be the comrade of those three youths whom Parthia's wrath, itself hotter than any flame, hurled into seething flames to punish their contempt for its power. As that story goes, two fires blazed up with equal but opposite heat; fury burned on one side of them, faith on the other, as a gentler fire did service for the holy youths and its coals shimmered with a tepid glow. In the end the astonished Parthian monarch saw all the fires he had kindled draw away. Later, Daniel and his similar valor equaled them in brave deeds and quieted the frightening mouths of the raging lions. Animals set afire earlier by goads of hunger and madness, their jaws restrained, now stretched out on the ground. Although hungry, they licked at the food before them and did it no harm, even as Daniel himself took his meal. It was carried to him by one of the prophets, who, a burden with a burden, was carried aloft, and, hanging in a gust of wind, driven through the sky by an angel's steadying hand, as he trod upon the air beneath him without himself taking a step. And Daniel took the food that came down to him, marvelling that the platters from a distant land were still hot and kept their taste even in a foreign place.

Now the boy, Daniel, happened to see Susanna being forced onto the rack by an ignorant crowd, who had condemned her unheard and who were now all struggling to catch sight of the guilty death of a guiltless woman. All at once he dashed into the middle of the throng and reproved the hot-headed mob with his young voice. "Why," he asked, "in a crowd so large, will no one pass sober judgement on what had happened? Why does no freeborn citizen shout out that he will not rush into an execution that might be unjust?" The crowd was immediately touched by the boy's words and responded by curbing its zeal. He himself was chosen judge and asked to assess the old men's guilt. Through him the way to truth was opened up. He took to one side each of the two men involved and asked them how the crime had taken place. Each one replied in a different way and so they confessed to the criminal pact by the discrepancies in their stories. Then a fearful anxiety took hold of all who were present as well. Shouts rang out on all sides, and the entire crowd fell upon the perpetrators of the crime. And they praised God Who never fails to hear the prayers of the just and Who makes His aid manifest when the time is right.

She, however, comes before even these women who with virgin modesty preserves her body inviolate in accordance with a heavenly vow. For if the universal judgement of mankind affords so much praise to the girl who is wed in accordance with the laws of this world, who guards her marriage bed and knows only one mate, just imagine how great a reward is ordained for a virgin's merits in that place whither Christ will summon us from here, when in His celestial home the Ruler of the world divides the human race into parts, promising salvation to His sheep but condemning the goats to an unpromising doom. Then angelic choirs will stand beside Him, admiring and praising the deeds of the good. Then the common debt of our fallen flesh will be manifest to all. No guile will be able to hide in the darkness, nor will it be possible to conceal the guilt all will know. Then your entire substance, your life itself will be examined to determine how rich the just Judge will make you with the rewards He grants. Our Teacher once summed this up in a few words. It happened that one day while Martha busied herself with her duties as a diligent servant should, because of the power of the Lord's word a care greater than that for food but which merits eternal nourishment held the attention of her sister. At that moment Martha uttered hollow complaints to the Lord. "Teacher," she said, "do You not see that I am taking the trouble to prepare this meal all by myself and that this sister of mine offers no help?" And Christ replied to her,

"There are many things which can hold you fast, but the better thing has been chosen by Mary, who is not caught up in the world's work, and this, which is the best portion, cannot be taken from her."

And so, my sister, while the world is on fire with its own concerns, never stop preserving the role you have chosen. All of your family have earned the right to claim you as their leading patron. We follow you now as our standard bearer, and the descendants of your parents are happy to attend you as you carry the banner of Christ. The world may have granted ancient honors to some of them and may continue to proclaim their noble descent in the titles it confers, but it graces even more those who bear God's ensign, for in their own right they have deserved their holy seats. I shall not at this point remind you of all your grandparents and great grandparents whose celebrated lives made them worthy priests. Look at your father who was selected to be a bishop. Just as he and your uncle, both of whom were pre-eminent in every way, after carrying the burden of public office, gain your admiration by taking on the burden of serving God's people, so now, my sister, lift up those humble brothers whom the Church has linked in a fellowship of vocations with their fathers and bound with similar obligations. On their behalf never tire of giving unending thanks to Christ or of pouring forth tears, so that none of your brothers will be missing from your family's number when you receive rewards worthy of your deeds and, having become the spiritual mother of your own forebears, you are joined in victory and joy with their virgin company.

# Index of Proper Names

# Select Bibliography

What follows is a brief list of editions and other works the reader may find useful. To these let me add several notes. First, the edition of Peiper remains the most reliable and complete, but readers may find the notes in Nodes' recent edition of books 1–3 useful as well. Peiper's edition includes an appendix that contains a list of both scriptural sources and poetic models. On Avitus' Latin, Goelzer and Mey are most helpful. On biblical paraphrase, Kartschoke provides a broad overview. Unfortunately Herzog's more detailed work is not complete. There are, however, a number of useful references to Avitus in the first volume. For the doctrinal implications of the poems, Nodes may be consulted. Finally, for a discussion of biblical paraphrase and the poetics of late antiquity, the works of Michael Roberts are recommended.

## Editions

*Opera quae supersunt.* ed. Peiper, Monumenta Germaniae Historica, Auct. Antiqu. 6.2. Berlin, 1883.
*Oeuvers complètes.* ed. U. Chevalier. Lyons, 1890.
*Opera omnia.* ed. Sirmond, 1943, reprinted in Migne, *P.L.* 59.
*De mundi initio*, BK I. ed. A. Schippers. Amsterdam, 1945.
*Avitus, The Fall of Man, De spiritualis historiae gestis, Libri I–III.*, ed. Daniel J. Nodes. Leiden: Brill, 1985.

## Other Works

Goezler, H. and A. Mey. *Le Latin de Saint Avit.* Paris, 1909.
Herzog, R. *Die Bibelepik der lateinische Spätantike*, vol. 1. Munich: Fink Verlag, 1975.
Kartschoke, D. *Bibeldichtung: Studien zur Geschichte der epischen Bibelparaphrase von Juvencus bis Otfried von Weissenburg.* Munich: Fink Verlag, 1975.

McDonough, C. J. "Notes on the Text of Avitus." *Vigiliae Christianae*, 25 (1981): 170–73.

Nodes, D. J. *Doctrine and Exegesis in Biblical Latin Poetry.* Liverpool: F. Cairns, 1993.

———. "Avitus of Vienne's Spiritual History and the Semi-pelagian Controversy. The Doctrinal Implications of Books I–III." *Vigiliae Christianae*, 38 (1984): 185–95.

———. "Further Notes on the Text of Avitus." *Vigiliae Christianae*, 39 (1985): 79–81.

Ramminger, J. *Corcordantiae in Alcimi Ecdicii Aviti Carmina.* Hildesheim: Olms-Weidmann, 1990.

———. "Zu Text und Interpretation von Avitus' *De spiritualis historiae gestis.*" *Wiener Studien*, 101 (1979): 313–25.

Robbins, F. E. *The Hexaemeral Literature: A Study of Greek and Latin Commentaries on Genesis.* Chicago, 1912.

Roberts, M. "Rhetoric and Poetic Imitation in Avitus' Account of the Crossing of the Red Sea." *Traditio*, 39 (1983): 29–70.

———. "The Prologue to Avitus' *De spiritualis historiae gestis.*" *Traditio*, 36 (1980): 399–407.

———. *Biblical Epic and Rhetorical Paraphrase.* Liverpool: F. Cairns, 1985.

———. *The Jeweled Style.* Ithaca: Cornell Univ. Press, 1989.

Roncoroni, A. "L'epica biblica di Avito di Vienne." *Vetera Christianorum* 9 (1972): 303–29.

# ⟨ᴅ⟩RTS

ᴍᴇᴅɪᴇᴠᴀʟ & ʀᴇɴᴀɪssᴀɴᴄᴇ ᴛᴇxᴛs & sᴛᴜᴅɪᴇs
is the publishing program of the
Arizona Center for Medieval and Renaissance Studies
at Arizona State University, Tempe, Arizona.

ᴍʀᴛs emphasizes books that are needed —
texts, translations, and major research tools.

ᴍʀᴛs aims to publish the highest quality scholarship
in attractive and durable format at modest cost.